SELINE'S WORLD

Humorous short stories for a grey day

ERIC MCFARLANE

My thanks to the enthusiastic members of West Lothian Writers for their invaluable advice, criticism and support.

You can follow Seline on facebook. She'd love to hear from you. Just search for Seline Allbright.

Seline's Little Flutter

My name's Seline, that's Seline Allbright, and I've decided I'm going to win the lottery. I mean I need a new coat to make up for the one the monkey did its business on, and new coats are expensive, because I'd like a nice one, not one of those cheapy things from Lidl. So if I won the lottery I'd have lots of money to buy a coat and maybe have enough left over to go on holiday to one of those erotic places like Greece or Cyprus or maybe even Brighton.

I told Senga about my grand plan. Senga, she's my best friend and she said that I would have to buy a ticket. She was right of course. She's always right. She reads books and knows things about stuff that people like you and me have never heard off, like space stuff and recipes for playdough. So I always listen to her. Mind she's not always right, she did once tell me our local councillor was a vegetarian and I know for a fact that he's married with three kids, but I didn't like to contravene her.

"Are you sure about this, Seline?" she said. "You know what it says in the bible about gambling, don't you?"

I said I didn't and she said neither did she, actually, so it was probably OK. I mean someone always wins so it's not a gamble is it?

Mind I don't want to win millions. I wouldn't know what to do with millions. I only want enough for a coat and maybe a holiday. Two holidays. I'd take Senga of course. She was really pleased when I said I'd take her on holiday and she went to the travel agent and brought back this big armful of brochures and started talking about where we would go. She put on her funny face when I said I'd have to win the lottery first.

They say money changes people but I'm not so sure. "Money won't change you Seline, a bloody earthquake wouldn't change you," Senga said. I thought that was nice of her. So they are wrong about money. Mind they're wrong about lots of things. They told Mam she'd die if she didn't give up those big black cigars of hers so she gave them up and then went and died anyway just to spite them.

Senga told me I could get a ticket in the newsagent round the corner, "Oh and bring me back an ounce of shag while you're there luv," she said. She has this big curvy pipe that her Uncle Roddy used to smoke before they took him away. "It's all I've got left of him," she once said to me, "that and his old breeks, and you can't smoke them."

I popped round at lunchtime to the newsagent and they were closed for lunch. You don't find many places closed for lunch nowadays do you? No one has time to eat lunch, they're all too busy doing stuff. So how come everyone's getting fat? It meant I had to go to the big newsagent down High St, you know the one, next to Jenkins the butcher. He calls himself a family butcher. I think that's funny, you know, like he butchers families and puts them in steak pies and other meat products. Like that Sweeny Todd fella' I read about. I don't mean butchering families is funny, just the idea of him calling himself a family butcher and not doing that. If I ever pass there with Senga I always point that out. She doesn't laugh, she doesn't seem to get the joke no matter how much I explain it. It's not that she doesn't have a sense of humour, she laughs at lots of things, even some things that aren't funny but she doesn't seem to get the family butcher joke, mind Mr Jenkins didn't get it either when I pointed it out to him.

So anyway I went into the newsagent. There was a queue at the desk so I had a browse around first. It's a big shop and they sell all sorts there. I love liquorice so I wasn't going home without a packet. They also have loads of books and magazines and DVDs and those computer game things that everybody plays. Some of them look really good but I'd have to buy a computer first for to play it. You

2

stick a disc in one of the slots and then do stuff with your keys and mice. Senga says it's not my scene but I'm going to try it sometime.

A woman standing beside me gave me a funny look and moved away. I must have been talking to myself. I know I do that sometimes but I just can't help it. I blame living alone or maybe it's something in the water.

By the time I'd wandered round the shop a bit the queue had gone down some, in fact there weren't hardly anyone in the shop.

"Can I help you?" The assistant was only a young girl. She was smiling but looked a bit jumpy, perhaps it was her first day and only the day before this day she'd been in school sitting behind a cosy desk and now she was cast out to face the world alone, and bring home enough money to keep her aged mother and disabled father from the workhouse. She'd be an only child too and wouldn't have any brothers or sisters to help with this task.

"Can I help you?" She wasn't smiling now.

"I'm so sorry," I said.

"Is there anything I can do for you?" She really sounded like she was working under strain.

"Oh contrayer," I said. "If there is anything I can do for you, you only have to say. I would be happy to help."

"We shut at 5.30," she said.

I looked at my watch. "It's only 1.30 now."

"Exactly," she said.

"Ah, you mean it's going to be a long afternoon for you?"

"Some are longer than others. Look did you come into the shop to buy anything?"

"Of course I did, luv." She was acting a little silly now, why else would I go into a shop for heavens sake. "I'll have these Allsorts and I was looking for one of them lottery tickets."

"At last," she said.

"Yes... at last." This conversation was getting a bit odd for me but she was the only assistant serving. I'd seen one of the others slipping through a door at the back.

There was a long pause. "So, how many tickets would you like, then?" she said.

"Oh, just the one, luv. I only need enough for a coat and a wee bit over maybe. I'm not greedy. I wouldn't know what to do with a lot of money."

"You want one ticket because you don't want to win too much?" She was taking a close look at the ceiling. Probably checking to see if the cleaners had done their job.

"There's a spiders web in the corner," I said. I'd seen it earlier on when I was walking round the shop. "And I'm not too sure about your windows."

She was staring at me with one of those looks that people get before they're seasick

"OK, OK one ticket," she said and she moved over to her big machine. "Do you have numbers?"

Numbers? What was the blessed woman talking about? Numbers of what? She might have meant anything. I was getting just a bit worried about her. And then I thought maybe she was foreign and didn't understand me, mind she didn't have an accent.

"I don't quite understand you," I said. "Are you from Poland? I can speak slower."

"Lucky dip then," was all she said.

I really didn't know what to say to that but at long last she pressed buttons on her machine and out popped my ticket.

"That'll be two pounds altogether." She whacked the ticket down on the counter so hard that two Quality Street triangles fell off their display.

I opened my purse and then I remembered. "Oh, and I need some shag," I said.

She stared at me again and her face went all red like a baby plum tomato from Morocco that they sell in packets in the supermarket.

"Please, do you have any shag?" I looked past her and I could only see cigarettes. "Just an ounce. My friend has a roller."

"Yes, I'm sure he does," she said. She had moved as far away from the counter as she could and was waving at a big man by the door.

He came over and they whispered to each other so that I couldn't hear which was very bad mannered of them. Manners maketh the man stroke woman I always say. Then the woman put her hand up to her mouth and stared at me again. I thought she was going to be sick. They both came over.

I had a quick rummage in my handbag. "I've got a plastic bag here, luv, only it's not very big. How sick are you?"

They both looked at each other. "I'm sorry, madam," said the man, "but we don't sell loose tobacco. There's no demand for it."

I thought of telling him there was and I had but I gave up, put my money on the counter and took my ticket. I wasn't going back to that shop, they were seriously loony.

When I got home there was a letter for me, and do you know what? My premium bond had come up, fifty pounds, so I can get my coat now. I don't need their silly lottery ticket. Senga said I should take it back to the shop for a refund and then she said she was just kidding, but you know, it's a good idea, I might just do that.

Seline and the Séance

or One Medium Fried

It was Senga's idea. "D'you fancy going to a séance, Seline?" she said.

She'd seen it in the paper, just below the ad for the new carpet shampoo - *Madam Pommefrit will perform a guided séance on Tuesday night*, it said. *Donation requested.* Senga's my best friend and she's like that, impulsive. She just gets an idea into her head and it's got to come out somewhere. She has too much in there, I reckon. I remember the lady who took the cookery class we went to last year said that Senga was fairly clever, and she should have known; she was a teacher cookery lady after all. In fact I found out later she was a lecturer so that proves it, doesn't it? About Senga, I mean. She's always telling me to do this or do that and not do other things what I want to do but I don't mind, she's not bossy, it's just her impulsivosity coming out. Anyway, I said that yes I would like to go to a séance, and what was a séance anyway, and would there be snacks? So she told me all about séances and it seems it's about people contacting their relatives and friends who've gone over to the other side so that they can ask them questions about what it's like over there and whether they're happy or not and even who's going to win at the gee-gee's. Fantastic I thought, I can ask about Mam.

I miss Mam such a lot since she left us. It happened so suddenly, one minute she was sitting in her chair by the fire stuffing her pipe with shag and the next there she was - gone. It's not been the same since. All the family miss her especially Uncle Bill. Mam told me he wasn't my real uncle but I always call him that just the same for respectfulness. When I was littler he used to come round Friday nights for his 'little bit of cheddar' although I don't know where he found it 'cos I like cheddar and I couldn't never find any in the fridge. I said he should try some of Tesco's brie for a change but he just looked at me kind of funny and asked what I was doing Sunday.

The séance thing was at 7pm so Senga and I had an early dinner, then she had a quick drag on one of her big black cigars, "Just to settle me innards like," she said, and we got the bus in good time.

I was sure it would be in some fancy hall but it turned out to be in a block of flats off the high street. It was up two flights of stairs and there was a big man holding a box at the door.

"Donations, ladies," he said and rattled his box under Senga's nose.

I could have warned him that it was a bad idea. Senga does not like having boxes rattled under her nose as the Salvation Army gentleman would tell you, if he could. And in addition to the rattling with the box he sounded very rude.

Senga pulls herself up and looks him in the eye, or she would have done if he hadn't been ten feet tall, but she did stare up his nostrils very fiercely. She told me about them later "It was like a bloody jungle in there," she said.

Anyway the man stares down at her and she says, "What?"

"I said donations, darling," he said, and rattles his boxy again.

"I understood that this was a free event," she says all posh like. She can go very posh when she wants.

He stares at her down his nose and bends over a bit so he can be sure she's really there. "It is free, that's why I'm looking for donations, dear."

"So these donations are voluntary then, son?"

"Yeah, voluntary, right."

"Good, well me and my friend here choose not to volunteer."

He made a growling noise in his throat but right that minute a couple appeared at the top of the stairs, the man dropped a tenner into the box and the big guy smiled at them. Senga grabbed my arm and pushed me through the door behind the couple as they went in.

It wasn't a very big room and it was almost dark with the curtains drawn. There were about twenty chairs and at the front a small table. There were three or four people there already and Senga and I sat at the back.

It was almost sixteen and a half minutes later when a lady appeared at the table. I say appeared but I wasn't actually looking when she did on account off I was listening to one of Senga's long stories about her dentures so I can't be sure that she didn't just walk in through a door but all of a sudden, there she was.

"Good evening ladies and gentlemen. I am Madame Pommefrit your guide for our journey tonight. I say journey...."

"You're late." I called over to her.

She looked up. "What? Excuse me?" she said.

"I said you're late." I was just worried that she might not realise she was late and maybe run over her time or something and not be back home to read her kids their bedtime stories.

"Unfortunately, my dear, the traffic was heavy and even I cannot..."

"You can always wake them up. I'm sure they wouldn't mind. For their Mum and all."

She stared at me for a long time and then shut her eyes for a longer time still. When she opened them she didn't look at me but made a kind of wavy gesture with her hands.

"Waking them up. That is exactly what we shall attempt to do tonight. It is a difficult path but the spirits are willing if we are. We all have someone we wish to contact, someone dear to us who has passed over to the other side. That question we never asked is forever there in our hearts and tonight you may ask it. Tonight you will ask it."

Then she spread her arms out and brought her hands in close to her head. "It is time," she said, and her voice went all low and whispery.

"I see pain," she announced. "Real pain. Does that mean anything?" Lots of people murmured. "I hear noise." More murmurs.

"Do I smell smoke?" The lady in front of me let out a gasp. "Yes, smoke there is, and perhaps flames. Could that be right?"

"It's my Ernie," the woman screamed. "He died in a fire, last year."

Madame Pommefrit put her hand up. "Wait... He says how are you? And the family? How are they?"

"Fine, fine. Tell him we're all fine, please," gasped the woman.

"I have my dear. Now is there anything you would like to ask... Oh wait, sorry. He has to go. He's fading. What was that Ernie? Oh yes. He says he will be back, my dear, and you must not worry. He is very happy." She lowered her head for a moment.

"Wow, that's incredible ain't it Senga," I said. "I never knew how easy it was to get in touch."

Senga made a humphing noise which she does when the sport comes on telly. But Madame Pommefrit was talking again.

"And now for some reason I am seeing the sea, a great wide sea."

I nudged Senga, "It's Mam. It must be." I jumped up and waved. "Yes, yes," I said. I could see Madame whatsit's eyes rolling in her head.

"Wonderful," she said. "Anyone else? No? Oh well. Do I see waves?"

"Probably," I said. "It's the sea."

Her eyes were shut. "Does the departed have a connection with the sea?"

"Yes you're right," I said. "She went on a ship. We all cried when we heard, especially Uncle Bill. He misses his cheddar."

"A tragedy. Wait... I think... yes, she's coming through. Ah I see now. It was a terrible loss, the ship went down so quickly."

"Sorry?" I said

"She wants you to know she didn't suffer."

"Well I know she didn't suffer."

"Well one can never be sure."

"I can so," I said.

Madame thing was looking quite cross. "Oh, is that so? And how can you be so sure?"

"Well I got a postcard last week."

She seemed to sway very slightly from side to side. "A postcard? From the dead?"

"Oh she's not dead, don't be silly. She writes regular. Doesn't say much, mind."

"But you said she drowned."

"Did not. She just left see. I was down the shops and when I got back there was a little note on a piece of paper, pink it was. She said, 'I can't stand it no more, Seline. Strains too much, luv, no offence. I'm off somewhere hot. You'll manage fine but you watch out for Uncle Bill now.' So I didn't take offence and I've been looking after Uncle Bill. He's round my bit a lot. Then two weeks later we gets a postcard from Majorca or was it Mexico? I remember it began with an M. Might have been Rome or something. And it said that it was hot and she wished I weren't there which was fine 'cos I wasn't."

I stopped then because there was a bang what made me jump. Madame Pomme-pomme had just left and slammed the door.

"She is such a rude woman ," I said to Senga. "I was just explaining."

"So you were love, so you were."

And you know all the way back home Senga was he-hawing fit to burst. We had to stop twice so that she could take her puffer. Well if that's a séance you can keep it. We didn't even get snacks.

Seline at the Library

Aren't libraries great? Have you ever been to one? You can pick up anything there, videos, newspapers, computers, adverts for street walkers, or rather dog walkers, and even books sometimes.

It was my friend Senga asked me to return the book she'd just finished. *Twentieth Century Poisons and Poisoners* it was called.

"Not feeling too good, luv. Think I'll take a wee lie down," she said.

But when I left she was rummaging through the kitchen cupboards and muttering to herself. It didn't matter because I'd already had a look and decided that a book would come in handy.

We've got a nice new shiny library with doors that open by themselves, sometimes. It's all glass at the front so you can see inside and look at all the people reading and doing other library type things. It's fascinating. I stood staring in for ages at an old man in jeans sitting reading a newspaper. Eventually he looked over and put a cheery finger in the air. I gave him a smile and a thumbs up.

I went inside and left my book on the counter where the nice looking librarian man was talking to another customer. He was bound to find it and stamp it for me with his stampy thing what puts the date on, or maybe that's when you take it out. Well he would know. Anyway, he had a nice face and glasses.

I decided to look around while I was there for a suitable book to use and maybe even one to read and help me get to sleep at night. Do you have trouble getting to sleep at night? I do. I never used to but now I sort of doze off thinking about Big Brother or Gordon Brown or some other programme and then I wake up all hot and can't get back to sleep. I blame global warming. Senga says I should switch off the electric blanket but if I do that my feet get cold and you can't sleep with cold feet now can you? Not until the globe warms a lot more.

There were a lot of computers all along one wall with people sitting staring at them. I looked over a young man's shoulder to see what he was doing.

"Excuse me," he said.

I think he must have made a smell. "It's all right, luv, it's natural," I said. "I'm a woman of the world."

It's never worried me. I mean everyone does it, just like drinking tea, or coffee. Some people prefer coffee, you know. I suppose it comes from growing up with Mam. She did a lot of it and I don't mean drinking tea, or coffee. Actually she never drank coffee. "It's a foreign drink, Seline," she'd say. You stick with good old British Ceylon, you won't go wrong," and then she'd let off a ripe one.

It was my boyfriend Terry started me on coffee when I was just left school. He thought it was sofishticated, he said. He meant sophisticated, but he worked in the fishmonger's, see, and I was never sure whether he was joking, so I didn't like to say nothing.

I had a look round the bookshelves for a book. It was ages until I found one that looked just right. I took it to the counter with the nice glasses man for stamping.

"I'll take this one," I said handing him my book.

"That looks interesting," he said.

I looked at the cover -100 ways to stuff your organic courgette-"Yes, it's about organic courgettes and the stuffing of them," I said.

He stamped the book. "I love healthy food. Grow your own do you?"

"Grow my own what?" I wasn't sure what he meant. "Senga rolls her own, but I'm trying to get her to stop. Everyone says it's very bad for you but then everything is these days isn't it except that Des O'Connor. He wouldn't be bad for you would he?"

He coughed a bit. "I think he's dead."

"Is he?" That was a shame. I'd always wanted his autograph.

"I meant grow your own courgettes."

Grow my own courgettes. What on earth would I want to do that for? "I'm sure it would be lovely to do that, dear, but I don't have a garden see, so I can't grow nothing. Mind Senga says I'm growing whiskers. Do you think I'm growing whiskers? Anyway what is a courgette?"

The poor man was looking a little pale.

"What is a courgette?" he said.

At first I thought he was being cheeky, repeating what I said like that, but he looked really unwell so I made allowances.

"I don't know, luv but you can look it up in your books and computers and things can't you if you really want to know? Senga would know. She knows everything about everything including stuff other people don't know. I don't know how she does it just sitting in that chair of hers, mind she does watch a lot of television."

There's a lot of education stuff on now have you noticed? There's that Richard Attenborough manny with his birds and bats and stuff. And Richard and Judy they got things that tell you about stuff. That's two Richards. Maybe they're related having the same name. That would be funny. And then there's Mastermind, that's good and yon phone a friend programme. I know lots of the answers on that.

"Hello, excuse me," The man was waving his hand in front of my face. "Are you sleeping?"

"There's no need to wave you're hand in front of my face, young man," I said. "I could be your mother or maybe perhaps your aunty or other relation so you just keep your hands to yourself."

Men are like that with their hands. They're everywhere. Uncontrollable they are. Mam warned me. - If he's fresh just grab his hands Seline and don't let go- good advice. I remember Vernon, a boy I knew from school. He worked at the shoe shop.

Come on round tonight Seline and I'll give you a fitting, he said. I did but he'd forgotten his measuring thing, he said, so he had to do it by hand, he said. It was OK on the feet but then he must have thought he was measuring me for a dress because...

"There's a queue here."

Someone behind me had spoken quite roughly, shouted even. I ignored him. Nothing that's shouted is worth listening to, I always say. The librarian was lying at his desk with his head in his arms. He looked like he might have been crying.

"Excuse me but are you all right?" I said.

He might have nodded but I couldn't be sure.

"You look ill. Do you need help." He didn't say anything.

"I'm a first aider. I did a course. I could give you the kiss of life. I was very good with the dummy." Well that worked. He jumped up like he'd been jolted by one of those heart machines that make you jump up like you've been jolted by... something or other.

He grabbed my book and stamped it again.

"Please," he said. "There's a queue."

"Well I can see that," I said. "You're obviously understaffed here. You need to employ more stampers for the stamping."

He said he definitely, definitely would, so I left him.

When I got home, Senga was still in the kitchen with a whole lot of little bottles and there was something cooking on the stove. It smelt good, perhaps she'd decided to make something for the both of us.

I took my book through to the bathroom and stuck it under the broken foot of the bath. There, a perfect fit. That would do until the man came to fix it.

Seline and the Shed

Well, it all started with that stupid shed of his. It took Percy three days to put it up in his back garden. Percy, he's my new neighbour. He's a bit strange. Anyway it looked just like a fancy shed, but you should have seen the concrete that went into it. He had one of those big noisy lorries with the turny thing on the back. It just can't be for a normal shed. And he wouldn't let me in.

"Can I help you?" he says, standing there with his hands on his hips as I went round the back of his house.

"Nice day," I said. Well I didn't want to give the game away.

"This is private property. My property," he says.

He had on a custard coloured tie and he was sweating like a loaf. You know when you get a hot loaf and you put it in a plastic bag and the inside of the bag gets all wet and the bread goes mouldy and you have to throw it out.

"I was just..." What could I say? I didn't want to tell him I'd been watching him from my bedroom window. "I was just admiring your tie." It was tucked into his trousers. I reached over and pulled out the end.

"Look... do you mind."

He tried to tug it back but I held on. I'm quite strong. "It's a lovely colour. Where did you get it?"

"Look, just stop. Give me my tie back. Who are you anyway? You've no right..."

He stopped speaking. He was staring at my eyes. People often do. They're different colours you see. One's blue and one's brown. Actually the brown one's a bit bloodshot. I showed it to the doctor on Friday. He gave me some eye-drops. I haven't used them yet.

They're in a funny bottle and you can't be too careful these days, what with those terrorists. He was definitely an Arab. He said he was from Wakefield but I'm not sure. Dr. Grant's off sick. Stress the receptionist said. It's a pity because I go to see him a lot.

"Seline."

"What?"

"I'm your neighbour Seline from just over there. Just past yon shed."

I tried to pull him towards the shed but he pulled back and there was a ripping noise.

"My tie. You've torn my tie."

"Sorry," I said, although really it was his fault he'd torn it.

"It was my best tie."

"Yes, it's lovely." I handed him back the end. "You should get it fixed."

"Fixed!"

"Sewed back together. Your wife will do it."

"I don't have a wife."

"Oh." I looked him up and down. He was really quite an attractive man if you ignored the sweating. Maybe a bit young for me but what did it matter. Nobody cares about age these days. I never got married see. Never bothered much with men. I mean not that there's anything wrong with them as such, it's just that they're so... you know. They only want one thing, Seline, that's what Mam used to say. Keep them in their place: out working and as far away from you as possible. Best marry a fisherman or the merchant navy, that way they're never at home and you can get some sleep. I did go out with a fishmonger once, but Mam said that didn't count. He did have lovely winkles though.

"D'you like fish?" I asked Percy.

"Fish? Are you mad?"

"There's nothing wrong with fish you know. They're good for the libretto."

Mam used to say to Dad, There's nothing like a fresh halibut to keep your pecker up. Then she'd turn to me and whisper, More's the pity.

"So if I take up singing I should attend Tesco's fish counter?" says Percy.

People say the strangest things. I mean what was he talking about? He was staring at me but I tried not to meet his eye. Did he regularly sing in Tesco?

"You do a lot of singing then?"

"None. I can't sing."

"My friend Senga's got a lovely voice. I'm sure she could teach you."

He put both his hands on top of his head.

"God in heaven! I don't want singing lessons. I just want a bit of peace in my own garden."

"Ah that's why you've got the shed then."

"It's not a shed. It's a summer house so I can come out here and get away from everything and everybody. But I see I'll have to put an electric fence round it."

I knew it. There was something about that shed. I mean why would you want an electric fence round a shed unless you had something to hide?

"Look," I said and pointed at the shed.

"What?" He turned round so fast he nearly tripped up.

"I thought I saw someone going into your shed."

"You're havering."

"Well possibly but I'm sure I saw someone furtive."

"Furtive?"

"Yup."

"But nobody's passed us."

"They have ways. You'd be surprised. Senga..."

I watched as he strode towards the shed. He was really very dishy. He must be all muscly under that jacket. I began to feel a bit wobbly. Perhaps he was the one. Senga says there's someone for everyone. You've just got to keep looking and remember that he's looking for you too. Mind she's not found hers yet. Or perhaps he hasn't found her. Perhaps they're both looking in the wrong place. Well maybe he was mine. My somebody. I mean I'm not getting any younger although I do use evening primrose oil. It's supposed to do all sorts of good things for you. Gets rid of wrinkles and keeps things going and it does a lovely job of the chips. I followed him towards the shed.

He was peering inside muttering to himself.

"It's not level," I heard him say. "The idiots."

"Excuse me," I said.

He turned to me. "The floors not level. You just can't get a good tradesman. Look, see for yourself." He stepped back and tried to usher me in.

Well I wasn't having any of that. Not just yet anyway. I hardly knew him, but I knew what he was after.

"We've hardly been introduced," I said.

He stared at me in a funny sort of way, like the way I saw Senga staring at the postman after he'd asked her to sign his autograph book.

"Oh, we haven't been introduced? Well pardon me. Percival Sandeman Denbigh at your service Madam. And you are?"

"Seline Allbright."

He held out his hand and we shook.

Oooh. His hand was warm and soft. I squirmed. And such a polite man. No one's ever called me Madam before. And I don't have a middle name. I guess Mam couldn't think of one. It was the war you see, rationing and so forth. What a man: handsome, polite and rich. You'd have to be rich to afford a shed like that. Could this be the one I thought? Well what the hell, I wasn't going to turn him down.

"Excuse me?" I heard his dreamy voice as if from a long way off.

"Yes," I whispered. "Oh yes."

"Could you let my hand go?"

18

"Oh, sorry," I said. Our hands were still clasped together. Entwined as they say in the stories. I gave it a squeeze.

"Please!" he said in a squeaky voice. It was one of those moments that you want to go on for ever, but I let go.

He let out a sigh of sheer contentment and stood there cracking his knuckles for a moment.

"All right," I said in my huskiest voice. "We can go in now."

"Pardon me?" he said.

I coughed to clear my throat. "We can go in now. I'd like to have a look at your... floor."

"Be my guest," he said followed by something I couldn't quite catch.

"So you see, Sergeant, I don't understand why he's complained."

Sergeant Barclay sighed and folded up his notebook.

"All right Miss Allbright. Now that we've had our little chat it's obvious that there has been a misunderstanding. I'm sure Mr. Denbigh will not press charges. But I must warn you that the restraining order does still apply. You must not approach within 50 metres of Mr. Denbigh's property."

I nodded. "I still think there's something funny about that shed."

"I've noted your comments from our earlier conversation, Miss Allbright. I assure you we'll keep an eye on things."

I felt badly let down. Percy had proved a major disappointment. Claimed he hadn't wanted to kiss me at all. Complained to the police that I'd molested him. Molested him! It was his fault he fell over and if I hadn't landed on top of him I might have hurt myself. Oh well. I guess he wasn't the one.

Sergeant Barclay stood up. Now there was a man. Why hadn't I noticed before. Tall, slim, lovely eyebrows, no nasal hair. Senga says if they don't trim their own they'll be asking you to do it.

"You'll be wanting me to report to the station, sergeant."

"No, no. That's perfectly all right."

"It's no trouble, honestly. I can come daily."

"If you want to report to the station Miss Allbright, then you do just that. I have work to do. Good-day."

Yes, I thought as the door shut behind him. You can keep your stupid shed Percy. It's down the nick for me.

Seline Goes to the Cinema

You know the way your belly rumbles after you eat a tub of coleslaw? Well that's what it was like for me last Saturday. I was at the pictures with Senga, she's my best friend like, and she nudged me and said, "Seline?"

That's me by the way, Seline, Seline Allbright, It's possible you heard of me, I wrote a letter to 'The Courier' about that Mrs Blair, Tina Blair, the woman what live down the bottom our road. She gets right up my nose see, don't even talk to me, just because I said she was a cow, I mean I said it in a joking way as one does but she took it all wrong. Anyway when I wrote the letter I didn't use her name I called her Mrs X – Mrs X Blair, I said and that she had been a horrible neighbour. So as I say, that's how you might have seen my name if they'd printed my letter, only they didn't print it so I wrote the editor asking why and they didn't print that either.

Anyway, Senga said, "Seline, your belly's rumbling again, you need to stop eating that stuff."

It was a real quiet bit in the film. 'Life and loves of an antique dealer', it was called, and this girl had called into the antique shop to ask the price of a silver sputum what she'd seen in the window and they'd kind of looked into each others eyes and discovered true love, as one does, and I think they were going to kiss each other or perhaps hold hands in a flirtatious way or something, when off it went – my belly that is.

Now I know we all have belly rumbles, I'll bet you do, but I have to admit mine are something special. They start very quiet, a bit like the bubbles in a fish tank and just get louder and louder, like they do when you stick your head in the tank. Everyone can hear, I know they can. Senga says if there was belly rumbling in the Olympics I'd be swinging that gold medal round my head.

"Look, I'm sorry," I said. "I just can't help it, you know that."

"You can so; you can stop eating that bloody muck for a start."

She meant the coleslaw. But I can't help it. I can't stand popcorn you see, it gets stuck in my teeth and everybody eats popcorn in the cinema and you do need something to eat otherwise you'd look strange so, me, I go to Tesco and get a big tub of cheese and chive coleslaw and that sees me through. I must admit it can be a bit messy though when it dribbles off your chin and down your cardie. I needed a hanky quick so I turned to the young man next to me.

"Do you have one," I said

He looked at me sort of strange as if I was a strange person or something and he said that yes, the last he'd looked he had one and what was it to me.

"Well," I said. "I just need it to wipe my chin."

He laughed and then he said *what?* And then he started kind of looking all round about as if he were lost. Well I gave up. I turned to Senga. "There's nowt so queer as folk," I said.

"You should know, luv," she said

But she gave me a hanky, and you know when I turned around the man beside me had gone. Well, good riddance I said to myself, him talking in cryptical remarks like that and all. He'd begun to worry me. He might have been one of those folk that go around talking to themselves and pulling faces a bit like our uncle Worthington.

Senga poked me in the ribs with her elbow and said, "It's finished," and blow me but the film was over and the music was playing and everybody was leaving.

"What happened?" I said.

"Typical bloody crap," she said. Excuse the language but Senga's a bit like that. Just opens her mouth and lets it all out. She doesn't put her words through the mincer first.

"But what happened, Senga? I was enjoying it and then that weird man kind put me off and all."

"Well she got together with the antiquated man, and he showed her a new use for a polished wooden golf club dating from the start of the nineteenth century, but it didn't work out and she stabbed him with a 1762 letter opener hallmarked in Birmingham. She got arrested and thrown in the clink and she hungs herself and when her guy recovered and found out he pined away and died and got buried in the same grave she was. It was a hoot."

I didn't know whether to believe Senga. It didn't sound like a hoot to me. But then sometimes she laughs in the wrong places when I tell her a joke so who knows?

Everyone had left the cinema but us and the people what clean up were kind of hovering around staring at us. I don't like being stared at, it makes me nervous. It all comes from our Miss Crivvens the teacher what we had at school when I was little. She used to stare at me a lot. I remember once during art we'd been asked to draw something we'd seen in the last hour. Well I was drawing away no problem when blinkety-blink there's Miss Crivvens stood staring over my shoulder at my drawing.

"And what may I ask, Seline, is that?" she said all funny like.

I looked at my drawing. "Well I'm not quite sure what it's called, Miss," I said. Which was true because I was just little then and I'd never seen one before. I know now of course, you see them everywhere – I blame the continentals. "It was Johnny Ingham showed me it at playtime, Miss. He bet me I'd never seen one like it before and I hadn't. Have you, Miss?"

There was a kind of strangly noise like you get when a chicken swallows a golf ball and when I looked up Miss Crivvens had turned bright red. Then she got very excited and dragged Johnny out off the class. I didn't see him again all week. I heard he got sent home with a letter for his Ma. I didn't really care, Johnny's the butcher's boy and he fancied me and he thought I fancied him but I never. He was just a pain. Mind you I did feel just a teeny little bit sorry for him, I heard he got big licks from his Ma and what he did wasn't that bad. I mean he shouldn't have brought it into school but it was interesting to see something new. You can buy them at the deli counter in Tesco now but way back then no one I knew had ever seen a salami.

Anyway I said to the ticket girl, what was staring at me. "Is there a problem, young lady, with you're staring eyes and what not?"

"Films dun," she says and all the time she's chewing gum like she's practicing for the Olympic chewing gum event, which by the way is being held in London this year I heard.

I looked at the screen. The music was playing and all the names were going up the screen. They were just thanking the Battersea antique dealers association for the loan of their letter opener.

"It clearly is not done," I said.

"S'credits." she says.

I turned to Senga, but she was busy digging earwax out her ear with a tissue.

"That's your opinion," I said to the gummy girl. "But I liked the film, or at least I would have if I hadn't been distracted by a strange man what was sitting here and distracting me with his remarkables. So I would like to see the end and what's more I like the music which is playing and which I could hear if you weren't here talking away over it. It was wrote by someone famous and if you look you will see who it was and be able to recognise his nice music again and enjoy it... and so on. Isn't that so Senga?"

"It's finished luv," said Senga. Then she held her tissue up to the light and tutted.

Well blow me, so it was. I stood up. "The film is finished now," I said to the girl. "So I and me friend shall be taking our leave."

She just stared at me with her mouth hanging open, but at least she'd stopped chewing that blessed gum.

"Honestly, Senga," I said as we left. "What do you make of that?"

"Spearmint," she said.

Seline and the Bank Robber

There was ever such a long queue in the bank. It stretched right to the entrance. I only just managed to squeeze in so I was rather close to the man in front. He turned round and stared at me.

"Excuse me," he said.

"That's OK," I said. I mean no-one can help it. It's quite natural. Some people get all embarrassed but it doesn't bother me at all. Mam's favourite saying was, 'Where e'r ye be, let the wind blow free.' She lived her life by that rule and it didn't do her any harm. Mind she didn't have many friends.

"Your umbrella," he said. "Would you mind moving it."

"Oh sorry," I said. I realised that my umbrella was poking him in the back pocket. The queue shuffled round a bit so I was able to move it.

"Thank you," he said in a very polite voice. He was very tall and wore a suit and tie with a briefcase in one hand.

"It was a pleasure," I told him. It always pays to be polite I find. He gave me a funny look and turned away

I tapped him on the shoulder. "It's a long queue."

"Yes, isn't it," he said.

"Not that I mind long queues. It's a good way of getting to know people. Complete strangers can be so interesting I find."

He muttered something that sounded like "sometimes," but I couldn't be sure.

"I'm Seline, Seline Allbright." He didn't hear me so I poked him gently with my umbrella.

"Seline," I said when he turned round. His face had frown lines on it. The poor lamb was probably exhausted. I expect he worked long hours in some office for not much pay with a boss who didn't appreciate him and now here he was queuing up in the bank when he'd rather be home with his wife and... I glanced at his hand. No ring, so perhaps he was single. But then people don't bother getting married now or even if they do they don't bother with rings so you can't really tell. It makes it very difficult. I wondered if he would wear a ring if he was married.

"Yes?" he said.

"You're quite right," I said. "Tradition's important don't you think?"

"What *are* you talking about?" He sounded really weary.

There was a comfy looking seat in the corner near the door. "Why don't you go and sit down," I said. "I'll keep your place in the queue."

"Well that's big of you."

"It's OK. I don't work you see, at least not in an office or whatever. I do plenty work at home of course. I've got a big house and I've got my hobbies. You should see my wooden fruit."

Well one minute he was there, the next he was gone. I didn't actually see him leave, I was thinking about my collection. I'm looking for a paw-paw just now. Everyone has apples and pears and so forth but you just try to find a paw-paw. I thought for a moment he had taken my advice about having a rest but no, he had gone. Just as well. He'd been a little too strange for my liking.

The queue had got very much smaller now. Time passes really quickly when you are enjoying a good intelligent conversation. People just don't have time for conversation these days, always rush, rush everywhere. That's what I like about my friend Senga, she sits and listens, mind, sometimes she falls asleep.

"Nearly there," I said to the woman in front of me. I gave her an encouraging smile. She looked really worried. I bet she'd been reading about yon bank robbery the other day when one of the customers got shot. It was all over the paper this morning.

"You're quite safe in here," I said. "No-one can get to you now." She was biting her lip and her eyes were looking everywhere. Thank goodness she was next in line, I couldn't have put up with her for long. I thought I'd better get my bank card out. It's a new one. I just got it last week. So I started to rummage in my handbag.

"Look," I said. "First it's you then it's me, OK?"

"Oh Christ no!" she screamed and rushed out the door like I don't know what.

The man behind the counter said "Next please," that was my turn.

I marched up to the counter and stuck my card under the little glass window thing that's supposed to stop him from being robbed. It's just a thin piece of glass. It would never stop a real robber, not one with a gun. He'd just shoot through it. Mind, perhaps it was bullet proof glass. I rubbed it with my finger but you can't tell. It didn't look very thick and it didn't say 'Bullet Proof' or anything on it. I gave it a tap with my knuckle.

The young man was saying something to me. "What did you say?" I said.

"I said can I help you, Madam?"

"Well yes, actually you can. I want to take out ten pounds and is it bullet proof?"

"Yes madam, I believe it is bullet proof. So I won't be able to shoot you, will I?" He smirked at me and made a noise in his throat that could have been a laugh. I stared back at him.

"I don't think you're supposed to shoot the customers," I said.

"You're quite right. There's a rule about it somewhere. Now can you put your card in the slot and then put in your PIN please."

I looked at him doubtfully. "My pin? Are you sure?"

"Yes your PIN. You have to put it in before you can get money out. I suppose you've forgotten it."

I didn't like his tone.

"Of course I haven't forgotten it. Where do I put it?" I said.

"Just in the keypad there."

I fished in my handbag. I always carry one of Mam's old hat pins see. Not that I wear a hat, I mean people don't these days in spite of all the cold weather caused by global warming. I've never understood that, why it gets colder when the globe warms. It doesn't make sense to me. Senga says you need to be a scientist to understand it and she's clever so she should know. Anyway, I carry the hat pin because of all these murderers and rapists you hear about. If one of them just looks at me it's out with the hat pin and stabby stabby goodbye murderer or rapist.

"Are you sure about this," I said.

"Yes," he said, but I don't think he was listening. He was staring at the ceiling and sort of humming to himself like he was trying to be a bee or perhaps a hornet.

I took the hat pin and stuck it into the keypad between the one and the two. Nothing happened so I pushed a bit harder and turned it a bit. Then everything happened at once. There was a flash and a bang and all the lights went out. Everyone was shouting, someone screamed and a bell started ringing.

I kept calm. Right, Seline I said, this must be a bank raid. I pulled the pin out and held it in front of me. There was very little light but I could see a man's shadow running towards me. He was shouting.

"Everyone outside, everyone outside please," so I stabbed at him with the pin.

"Holy shit," he said and ran away.

"Gotcha," I shouted.

Everyone was running for the door, customers and staff, so I followed them. There was a police car outside when we got out with its blue light winky-winking. Everyone was crowding round, and a lot of pedestrians had stopped to look. What a racket.

There was a man sitting on the ground. I had a suspicion I knew who he was. He had pulled his shirt up and was staring at his belly. He was talking to a friend. I sidled over all nonchalant like and heard him say, "Stabbed me right there..."

That was all I needed. It was him. I went straight over to the police car. There was a young policeman talking into his radio thingy.

"Excuse me," I said. "I know who the robber is."

"There's been no robbery madam. It's just a false alarm. We're investigating the cause at the moment."

"Oh yes there has been," I said. "And it was him over there. The one sitting down."

The policeman stared at the man. "I believe that's the manager, madam. We were just going to have a word with him."

"I don't care who he is. He's the one. He's the robber and he tried to rape me."

He stared at me for a moment then he looked at his colleague. The other one shrugged. "Better take them both down the road."

"Just wait right here, madam, while we go and see about this. And don't move."

He spoke very severely and he was a lovely handsome boy. I could have waited all day for him but I remembered I'd left the washing out and it was coming on to rain, so I thought I'd run home and rescue it. So I set off home. There was a lot of shouting from behind. The robber resisting arrest I suppose.

The washing was fine, nearly all dry, apart from my pyjamas, that's the red pair with the hazard warning sign on the front. Senga got me them for Christmas. They're cotton you see and they take ages to dry. The rain was off so I left them on the line and went in to make the tea.

When I got back to the bank there was no-one there, not a soul. I tried the door but it was locked. It was then I remembered that young bank clerk still had my card. Oh well, I suppose I'll have to go back tomorrow, but I'm going to keep my pin handy.

Seline at the Doctors

I had to go. I mean it was getting embarrassing, so I went down the surgery to see Dr Grant, on my way back from the abattoir.

"He's gone," says the receptionist.

"Oh dear," I said. "His poor wife."

"No, no, I mean he's left, left the practise."

Now that was a shame, I liked Dr Grant. He was really nice, always listened.

"Gone to another practise then, has he?" I said.

"Well no. Actually it was stress, I believe, He was really ill when he left. I think he's taking a sabbatical."

I was really sorry to hear that, drugs are such a menace these days. I suppose someone in his position would be able to get them real easy. "Well at least he's not on the coke," I said.

"Excuse me?" she said.

"Yes, of course, no problemo. You go right ahead. I'm not in any hurry."

I looked around the waiting room. It really was looking quite dingy. Needed a fresh coat of paint. A few pictures on the wall would brighten things up too. My friend Senga would do it. There's not much she can't do with a paint brush. She's very practical with her hands. She says I'm more the cerebral type. It means I do a lot of thinking and stuff like that.

"Hello. I said excuse me." It was the receptionist back from the bathroom.

"That was quick," I said.

"Quick? How d'you mean."

"Quick getting back from the bathroom."

"I haven't been to the bathroom."

"It's nothing to boast about. That's one of my problems."

She looked at her watch and gave a sigh. Perhaps it wasn't working.

"It's 2.30 dear," I said. "Give it a shake. I find that sometimes helps."

"Can I help you with anything," she says with her nose stuck in the air.

"I need to see a doctor," I said. "If Dr Grant's a junkie now I'd better see someone else. Who's his replacement?"

"Dr Grant is not... Dr Pickering has taken Dr Grant's place. Would you like an appointment?"

"Yes, that's what I'm here for," I said.

"Well I'm glad we've established that," she said in a funny sort of way. "Right how about next... no wait a moment there's been a cancellation. If you can wait he can see you in half an hour."

"Half an hour's fine for me, dear," I said. "I'm used to waiting. Do it all the time. Buses, queues, telephone so might as well wait for the doctor. Senga, she's my friend, she doesn't like waiting, gives her heartburn she says. If the bus doesn't come she just walks. Walked five miles once she did. She had to go for a lie down after. Now Mam..."

"OK, I'll put you down. Can I have your name, please?"

Really, I thought it was a bit rude of her to interrupt, but I didn't say anything.

"It's Seline, Seline Allbright, thank you."

She had started to write but stopped and looked at me in a funny way.

"Ah... you're the Allbright woman."

"Yes, do you know me?"

"Yes indeed... well no, not really." She coughed and went a bit red in the face.

I was disappointed but how would she know me when I didn't know her? Mind Senga says I'm well known. I don't know why. I mean I've never been in the papers or nothing. Well apart from that business at the take-away but that wasn't my fault or that stupid bank manager. He should have known better at his age. The receptionist was saying something.

"I said you can take a seat, Miss Allbright."

It was nice she'd got the Miss right. I get annoyed when people call me Mrs. I mean not that I've anything against people getting married and the rest of it and I've had boyfriends. Terry from the fish shop was the first. He said he would bring me round a nice bit of haddock he'd been saving all week just for me. It'll be off then, I said. Oh no he said it was just ready. I said fine as long as it was coated. And do you know what he tried to do that night? Well someone had the wrong idea that's for sure. I had to go for a take away after I'd thrown him out.

"I said you can take a seat, Miss Allbright."

The receptionist was pointing into the waiting room and she was looking quite annoyed. There was a bit of a queue waiting as well so I suppose she was getting harassed. Typical, a busy surgery and they don't employ enough staff just like banks and call centres and abattoirs.

"You need to get more," I said and went through to the waiting room.

It was really busy in there. I sat in a corner seat between two men.

There was a youngster with a baseball cap and an older man looking very serious. There's not much to do in a waiting room apart from wait so I did. I read a notice on the far wall about getting flu jabs for the winter. I got one just two weeks ago. I turned to the man beside me and said "Have you been done?"

He jumped like he'd eaten a frog. "What? he said. He'd gone all pink in the face.

"Done, have you been, this winter. I have."

"I... I don't understand," he says. I think perhaps he was from foreign.

"It's free, doesn't cost a penny. It really helps to know you won't catch anything nasty. Senga, my friend, gets it every winter."

"I'm sure that's nice for her," he said. He was squirming about in his seat like he had ants in his panties. "I think that's me called now," he said and jumped up and scooted off.

I hadn't heard anyone being called so I decided I would have to listen really carefully.

"Miss Allbright?" That must be Dr Pickering.

He smiled at me and held the door open as I went in, which was kind of him. He was quite young and broad-shouldered in a doctory sort of way. He showed me to a seat.

"Please take a seat," he said.

"Thank you, please do too," I said.

He sat down, put his hands under his chin and said, "Now then, how are you?"

Well what can you say to a question like that?

"Well doctor, there are a few problems."

"Tell me all about them," he smiles.

"Some of them are a bit embarrassing like."

"I can assure you, nothing you say will be new to me, Miss Allbright."

I decided to start with my toes and work upwards and so I did.

He asked lots of questions at first but then he got quieter. When I got to my knee joints he didn't say a word and when I started on my thighs he was looking at his watch as if he was in a hurry or something.

"Look, Miss Allbright, is there one particular area that's bothering you more than another at the moment?"

"Oh yes, it's the waterworks you see, that's why I came along today."

"What? But why didn't you... wait, Allbright? Seline Allbright?"

"That's right," I gave him my best smile. He moved a little backwards and started pressing buttons on his computer. He read something for a moment and stared at me again.

33

"Ah." he said.

"That's what the patient's supposed to say," I said.

"What?"

"Ah."

"Ah?"

"Yes."

He blinked several times as if he had a fly in his eye. I stared a bit closer but of course I was still to far away to see anything.

"I could get it out for you," I said.

"No," he shouted very loudly. "That won't be necessary."

"I've got a hanky." I pulled it out of my pocket. "It's nearly clean too. I just have to wet the corner."

"Please don't wet anything. No really, please."

Oh well if he was happy to have a fly in his eye why should I worry. He was looking quite flustered with it though.

"You say you have a urinary problem, please tell me about that, no wait, I think it would be best if you give me a specimen first, we'll send it away for testing. Can you do that now? You can hand it in later if you want."

Well ever since coming into the surgery I'd been dying to go which is just the opposite of my problem but there you are. So I said I could and he gave me a bottle thing and told me to go behind the screen. While I was there there was a very quiet knock at his door. I didn't know whether he had heard it so I shouted, "That was a tap at your door."

He says right back, "Don't worry I'll get the plumber." That was really weird, I couldn't figure it out. Why would he want the plumber? I was beginning to think... He opened the door and whispered for a moment. "I'll be right back," he said.

Well I put something in the bottle for him but when I looked there was just this tiny dribble there, it was never going to be enough so I topped it up with water at the sink. I put the bottle on his desk but I must have spilled a little because it left a yellow ring on his prescription pad.

He still wasn't back so I sat in his chair and had a quick look at his screen. There was all sorts of gobbledygook on it but I saw my name at the top. Underneath there was a section that said 'notes' and it was all in red. There were all sorts of medical words and Dr Grants name was at the end. I could have sworn I only pressed a few buttons to try and see some more but the whole screen went black apart from a little flashing 'C' at the top corner and 'format drive?' I pressed the enter key thing and it started humming to itself so I suppose it was ok.

There was still no sign of Dr Pickering. I wasn't sure what to do. I could have waited but I was getting bored and I'd left the specimen so I decided just to leave quietly. There was no one at the reception desk but as I passed I could see Dr Pickering in the back office sitting with a cup of something in his hands. That receptionist was bending over him and patting his back. Well really, there was obviously some hanky panky going on there and in full view of anyone standing on tiptoe. It's not right. I didn't like that receptionist, a gold miner that's what she was but he should have known better too him being his age and a doctor. I decided I wasn't going to have a man like that looking at my what-nots or even my what-evers. I just wouldn't be able to trust him. He might come over anytime with his unbridled rust and then where would I be? At his mercy that's what. I'm going to find another doctor.

Seline at the Seaside

Life was going nowhere. Senga and me were getting in a rut. So I was glad when she got her idea. We were sitting eating sardines from a tin, and I was just wishing I had a fork, when she suddenly brought it up - the idea I mean.

"We should go to the seaside, luv. I need to get out of town. I'm fed up with all the noise and smoke."

She was quite right. I hate noise too. It gets into your head and messes your brain up so you can't think straight. Just like desiccated coconut, all those little bits that get stuck in your teeth. I hate it.

Senga said she would drive us down the coast a bit to the beach. She's got this little yellow car. Only it's a bit too little really because she's got a lot bigger than she used to be. I don't say to her of course, I'm diplomatic, but she does eat too much.

When we got to the seaside the sun was shining and it was quite hot so Senga removed her hat, which she doesn't do very often, except when she's in the house and even then not always. "You just never know, luv," she says.

I said I would buy the ice-creams but when I got back she was talking to this old man she'd found by the waste bin. She gave me a big wink and whispered, "Think I've got a lumber here, luv. Look you go and do something and me and him will go for a wee walky like."

"You sure you know what you're doing, Senga?" I asked her. Of course there's no telling her, I knew that, once she's made up her mind that's it - made up.

I walked down to the beach and saw the rowing boats. All sorts of colours they were and £6 for an hour it said. I really fancied that. I used to go down to the duck pond with Mam when I was a girl and we would row for hours round and round while Mam tried to catch a duck. Sometimes she got one and she'd cook it for our tea. I love the smell of roast duck, that and porridge.

Anyway I gave the man £6 and he gave me a lovely blue boat. I rowed out into the middle of the bay where there were no other boats about and it was really peaceful. I could hear the birds and the gulls like what you can't hear when you're in the city because of all the cars and people shouting at you because they think you're deaf. I sat there for ages just daydreaming and then I woke up from my daydream and there was another boat floating over to my left or port as we say; only there was no one in it. There were no oars either. Right Seline I said, investigate.

I rowed towards the boat as fast as I could. When I was nearer I looked over my shoulder and you know; there was somebody in it. There was a pair of bare feet sticking up in the air. I was sure they were men's feet. You can tell. And then his bottom stuck up in the air and then disappeared again. He was half-wearing a pair of red shorts. The boat was rocking from side to side and he was thrashing up and down like he was in pain. I knew what he was doing of course.

He was having spasms. It comes from drinking seawater. You mustn't do it. I read about it in Uncle Vernon's encyclopaedia. He showed me it one day when I was over helping him with his cucumbers. Uncle Vernon was a sailor in the old days when they had sails and masts. "If there's one thing you should learn in life, Seline," he said, "Never drink seawater." I never have.

I shouted hello over to the boat but there was no reply. It really looked like he was in trouble. I rowed right up to it. The boat was fairly jiggling around in the water now.

The boats bumped together. The man looked up. I reached over, grabbed hold of his rowlocks and pulled hard.

"What..." he said like he was in a bit of a daze. It's the salt does it or perhaps heat-stroke. You just can't be too careful even in this country. Even when it's cloudy you can get sun burnt, I read that somewhere, not when it's raining though, at least I don't think so.

I could see now there was a young lady in the bottom of the boat. I think he'd been giving her the kiss of life. Perhaps he'd pulled her out of the water in a nearly drowned situation. The poor lamb had lost the top of her swimming costume and she was staring at me with a wild look in her eyes like she was all confused and didn't know what to do. I've seen that look before.

"Pete, what's going on?" Her voice was all high and hysterical, a bit like Olive, you remember Olive and Popeye? Well a bit like her.

"What the hell are you doing?" the man shouted at me.

"Don't worry now, I'm just here to help you," I said. I ignored the swearing. I mean I don't like swearing but you've got to make allowances. The poor man had just discovered that he and his friend were safe and would be able to continue with their lives and live to a ripe old age and maybe end up in a retirement home and be visited by their children with fruit, and on top of that there was the probable heat-stroke.

"What? Look I don't need help."

He jumped up then and started waving his hands about and making the boats rock and it was then he started to say some really offensive things. I'm not going to repeat them because they were not very nice and as I said I don't like swearing. Suffice is to say, as they say, that he compared me unfavorably to a four-legged animal that we get milk from.

"Pete, don't. Sit down. You'll have us over." The young lady had found the top of her swimming costume now. "Look, I don't know who you are," she said to me. "But honestly we're fine. We don't need help."

"You haven't any oars, you're drifting helplessly at the mercy of... things," I said.

"Oars," the man yelled. "I'll give you bloody oars."

"I have oars thanks, that's the problem for you," I said.

"Pete, no. Look Mrs. whatever-your-name-is. We have oars, right down here, look."

And bless me they did. Right down in the bottom of the boat.

"Ah, you've shipped them," I said.

"What?" they both said together.

"Shipped them, It's a nautical term for when you put your oars in a safe place for use at a later time."

The man wasn't calming down at all. In fact his face was going red and blotchy like one of those mushrooms you find in the forest. They're quite poisonous. Mam once cooked some mushrooms she found in the Bluebell Wood for Dad, but he was fine afterwards.

"Look, just, just, just...," and he said something that was *really* not nice and meant go a long way away and don't come back for awhile or perhaps never at all. Well there is a limit and that was it.

"All right, if you're going to be like that, I'm just going to leave you, to drift eternally and forever in your sea of troubles, so there." So I rowed away and left them. They both sat staring after me for a long time. I heard the young lady say that she wanted to go home which was a good sign but the man didn't sound too pleased.

I told Senga about it later and she had a good old laugh although I didn't think it was funny. I was still worried about that boy and girl. Senga told me the old man had been a disappointment. He took her for a fish supper only he didn't have any cash and she'd had to pay.

We were just coming out of the amusement arcade when I saw them again - the couple from the boat. They were walking along the street hand in hand. I gave them a wave and smiled. They both stopped dead. The girl put her hand up to her mouth and I think the man said holy shmoly. I wanted to make sure they were OK. I ran towards them and do you know they sprinted back down the way they had come like they'd seen a ghost or a large animal with many pointy teeth. I gave up. Oh well, at least they were safe.

Senga was all red in the face and wheezing when I got back.

"God love, you'll be the death of me. Where's me puffer?" she said.

She gets wheezy when she runs or laughs a lot. She had a couple of puffs and she was fine.

"Right, Seline, it's time we got you home before you save anyone else." I didn't really understand her because I hadn't saved anyone. I mean that couple must have rowed back themselves. Sometimes Senga says strange things. She's an enigma that's what I call her. Oh well, it had been an adventure. I felt much better for our little trip.

We squeezed into her little yellow car. We'd only been driving for a minute when she yells "Quick luv, wave," and she beeped her horn three times. I put my hand up and only just had time to see that we were passing the same young couple who were standing waiting at the pedestrian lights. I turned round to try and see them but I couldn't. Senga stared in her mirror for a long time. She had to stop in the next lay-by and have two more puffs of her puffer.

Mr Pemberton Goes too Far

I think he's gone too far this time. I mean you do have to be careful what you do, especially in public. You've got to keep up appearances. Just saying that makes me think of Mam, although she was the opposite. She never worried about appearances. Every Saturday night she'd be down the boozer arm-wrestling the men for pints. Sometimes she won and she got her pint. Thing was that even when she lost they usually bought her one anyway, or even two. So Saturday night she'd be steaming home up the high street. She had a lovely voice. It was kind of sopranoy only a bit bassy as well. I could have listened to her all night. Sometimes I did and all.

Uncle Bill used to go on about her and her singing. He didn't like it. Thought she was making an exhibit of herself. 'That mother of yours Seline, she'll be the death of this family.' Then he went and dropped dead himself at the races a couple of days later. It was very sad. A horse ran over him when he drank a little too much and wandered onto the course. There's a horse-shoe engraved on his headstone, not because he got ran over by one, just 'cos he liked the gee-gee's so much. I've seen it. It's quite touching and very tasteful.

Anyways that's what I mean about appearances. You've got to keep them up even in graveyards, that's what I was saying. Look I'll tell you a story, it's true mind. I can't be bothered with all this fiction stuff you get in the library. What's the point in reading about things that never happened when there's stuff happening all around. You only have to look, and they get paid for it too. Thousands of pounds for writing down stuff that never happened. Lies, Mam would have called it if she were alive today bless her. And then they swan of and sit by swimming pools in Bolivia and maybe have women there who aren't their wives and they do stuff what I've read about it in the papers and you probably have too - read about it I mean. My God, excuse me, it makes me so angry and there we are paying our taxes so that they can sit and proliferate with women who could be their daughters and should know better by swimming pools in Bolivia and probably women as well with young men cos women write lies too and... what was I saying? Oh yes, real stuff happening like what you see when you open your eyes.

Mam used to say what you don't see won't do you no harm. That's why she married Dad, she said, but I don't think that made a lot of sense. Senga, she's my best friend, sometimes goes around with her eyes shut. I mean really shut. She'll be outside and we'll be walking along talking about this and that and boyfriends sometimes and she'll just shut her eyes and try and keep going in a straight line, only usually she doesn't, she pushes against me and I push back to straighten her up only I might push too hard and she goes wandering into the road to the conflagration of vehicle drivers who may be passing at times and may toot in an unfriendly fashion at her. She just toots back at them only I don't suppose they hear her as she doesn't have a very loud toot.

What she does have is a loud voice, a voice like a stegosaurus the librarian said when we were in the other day counting the books. Senga likes to count all the books one section at a time. Like this week it was thrillers, next week it's Westerns and last week it was chicken-lit. She writes them all down in a little book with pink stripes on the cover. There were three hundred and fifteen thrillers if you want to know or even if you don't that's what it was. I asked her about it once and she said that one of these days the time would come and put her finger to the side of her nose. She's deep Senga is, very deep. She has wheelies within her wheelies. Now I don't ask her any more, I just help her count. I know there's a reason behind it all, I'm just not clever enough to see it.

Anyway the librarian wasn't very happy seeing as Senga was counting out loud and making a spectator of herself she said, so she asked her to be quiet. Senga stared at her and she stared back at Senga. I stared at them both. Senga's mostly quiet like but when she gets annoyed with people she can get all steamy. It was what you call a tender situation. I needed to do something.

"Can I use your toilet?" I said to the Librarian.

"What?" she said.

"Your toilet, can I use it?" I spoke a little louder. I think she was deaf.

"I... no, sorry, it's for staff only."

"I'll be very quick," I said. "It's a bit urgent."

"I don't think..."

"It's my bladder see. I had an operation last year. I have problems doing it and then when I do..."

"Yes, yes, yes. OK it's this way. I'll need to get the key. Just follow me please."

I gave a thumbs up to Senga as I followed the librarian round the corner. By the time I'd finished, Senga had gone which was my plan. I was just heading out the door when the librarian shouted at me in a very rude voice.

"Excuse me, the key?" she said.

"Yes, thank you," I said.

"Well can I please have it back."

I stopped in the doorway and thought really hard and you know, I couldn't think where I'd left the key. "It's in the door," I said.

It was a little white lie. I mean I really couldn't remember so it might have been in the door. I had a quick look through my pockets but the librarian was heading for the toilet so I thought I'd better run quick. You know I found that key two weeks later, it was in the drum of our washing machine. The repair man showed it me when he gave me the bill. I thought of taking it back to the library but decided not. Senga said I should take the bill to the library and ask them to pay as it was their key what broke the machine. I wondered if I would but then I'm never sure if Senga's kidding. Sometimes she says things all serious and then says she was only kidding. You're supposed to smile when you kid aren't you? At least that's what Mam always said. Keep smiling when you kid, Seline she said. Actually she didn't say that at all. I was just kidding, see, but I didn't smile, so you didn't know. I mean it's the sort of thing she might have said. She was always coming out with wise sayings and whatnot. Guff Dad called them which is what he called wise sayings.

Anyway, I was talking about appearances, keeping them up and so forth. Well I was just walking down the street see minding my own business and trying to look over Mr. Pemberton's hedge which he's let grow far too tall. I told him so last week. He said it helped keep pests out. I don't really see how it makes any difference 'cos they'll just crawl under it or fly over it but he seemed happy. Anyway I couldn't quite see so I dragged a milk crate over that was lying outside the paper shop. I left the bottles neatly at the side so no one would trip over them. and when I stood on the crate I could just see over the hedge. Well Mr. Pemberton was there and there was a woman with him only it wasn't his wife. She was a little curvy young lady in a short skirt. They were both on their knees in the corner by the water feature and he was planting his seeds. She was holding his dibber and he was popping them in quite the thing.

Well it wasn't right, she was young enough to be his daughter, mind maybe she was his daughter. But I know Mrs. Pemberton, she works down the post office and she's never mentioned a daughter so maybe it was his fanciful piece which wasn't right. That sort of thing just doesn't go on in our neighbourhood in broad daylight where anyone standing on a milk crate could see everything.

"Hello, Mr. Pemberton. I can see you," I said.

He looked up from his dibbling and did a kind off double take when he saw me. It must have been quite a surprise to know that his game was up.

"God, it's you," he said.

"Yes it is," I said.

"You've grown since I last saw you." I hadn't expected him to say that, but then what can you say when you're caught with your dibber in a comprising situation.

"No, I think you're mistaken," I said. "I am however standing on a milk crate."

"Ah now that explains everything, especially the current economic situation," he said.

I thought about that for a minute. I didn't understand what he was on about. Then I noticed they were heading for the back door and I realised he was just trying to distract me.

"Excuse me," I said. "We haven't been introduced."

"Oh dear, haven't we?" He stood there with his hands on his hips looking like a two handled teapot without the spout and with stripes because he had a stripy shirt. "Well I'm Mr. Pemberton and this is my niece Sally."

He turned to her and said, "This is Miss Seline Allbright, Sally."

She stared at me "Oh *that's* her," she said.

They didn't say another word, just went back inside and slammed the door so hard that the little gnome on the step fell over and chipped his beard. I could see in the back window a bit but then Mr Pemberton appeared and swished the curtains shut. There was nothing else to do. If I'd had a hedge trimmer I could have done his hedge for him but I didn't so I returned the milk crate to the shop.

It was all very confusing. I mean if she was his niece perhaps she really was just helping him, but nieces didn't look like that in my day, but then I suppose I was the same age as him so perhaps my age was his age but I still don't think she looked like a niece. I decided I would ask Senga what I should do. She's good with these things or maybe I would go and see Mrs. Pemberton in the post office and ask her about strange young women in her garden. I would have to be subtle of course, but that would be easy, it's second nature to me.

Seline Catches a Cold

It's so embarrassing when you get caught with toilet paper up your nose. It happened to me last Friday. I was round at Senga's place on account of she'd asked me to help her with her blocked sink. We were sitting down having a wee cuppa after we'd done some plunging with the plunger thing that unblocks sinks, only it hadn't and Senga said she'd need to get a wee man in for to do it, and since I'd had this really runny cold I'd stuffed some toilet paper up each nostril to stop it going, you know, into the tea and everywhere and making a mess and all and then the door bell went and it was the postman. I'd completely forgot about the toilet paper on account of I'd been listening to Senga going on about the wood louse she'd found in her tea cup, after she'd drunk the tea. It was lousy tea anyway she said and we were having a good laugh when the door bell went. I opened the door and it was a young man stood standing there.

"Package..." he said like he was going to say something else but didn't. That was all. He just stood staring at me.

"Yes," I said. "It's a package all right." He was holding out this parcel towards me but he seemed to be frozen just like a fish finger or perhaps a waffle in the freezer cabinet in Lidl's when they remember to turn them on.

I put my hand out for the parcel but he wouldn't give it me. I was getting annoyed with him. He was looking at me like I'd got horns or something.

"I don't have them, you know," I said. "I take them off during the day, so I don't scare people. I keep them under the bed." I thought that would make him laugh but it didn't. He just kept staring.

Finally he said. "You've got..."

That made a lot of sense, I don't think. And then he rubbed his nose with the back of his hand which was quite disgusting. Well if that was the sort of staff the post office was taking on now well no wonder they were having problems with their targets.

"I'm sure I wouldn't like to see what your percentage is like," I said.

He handed me the parcel then and backed away slowly. I closed the door on him sharpish and then had a quick peek through the letter box. He was still standing there and kind of muttering to himself. "You can go now. Your job is done," I said, through the letter box. He jumped and almost tripped on the top of the stairs in his hurry to get on with his round.

It was Senga told me I'd still got my pluggies in when I got back to the sitting room. She was hooting like an owl that had gone all hysterical.

"That poor boy," she said in between hoots, "he probably thought you were crazy."

I got a bit annoyed with Senga then, 'cos she wouldn't stop with the hooting and I was a bit embarrassed too. I mean if I'd remembered I'd have pulled them out earlier. Going around with tissue up my nose and frightening young boys isn't something I do every day. I told her I was going back to my bit for just now and I would see her at another time when she was less owly. I pulled out my plugs and left them in Senga's ash tray.

When I got downstairs I remembered I hadn't got any tissues with me so I had to keep sniffing all the time which was difficult and also problematical for me. I went into this little corner shop to get a packet. I was holding my nose now because it was really bad, running like a tap when it's left on and also stuck at the fully open position due to some problem with its internals which I don't really understand which was why you need to call a wee man in sometimes. There was a tall dark man behind the counter with a turban and a smile.

"Hello," he said. "What can I do for you, madam?"

Madam! Well that was a good start. I could tell we were going to get on fine. I mean sometimes you know before you even speak to someone that you're *not* going to get on with them. It happens to me all the time. I think I'm sensitive to oras. Everyone has an ora you know. I saw a programme about it on the TV. It was made by the BBC, or maybe one of those other channels, so it's true. Anyway they were on about the ora that everyone has and how you could detect it with the scientifical stuff that scienticians use for detecting oras and maybe other things. They showed it on a special screen that this person had a blue ora and this other person had a passion fruit ora. So I think I can detect these things in my unconscious mind where stuff happens that you don't know about. I remember telling Senga about it and she said she thought I would be sensitive because she didn't know anyone with a bigger unconscious mind than me. I thought that was a compliment but now I'm not so sure. I was feeling a bit in the huff with Senga just then.

So anyway I smiled at the tall man who was rubbing away at his beard and making some sort of gesture to the people who seemed to have joined me at the counter. It's funny, one minute a shops quiet and the next it's busy just like this shop. There's no accounting for it.

"I'm looking for tissues, please," I said. It was difficult speaking and holding my nose at the same time.

"I am sorry madam. We do not sell dishes in this shop. Only newspapers and chocolates and cool drinks."

I was sure I'd seen packets of them by the door but there were so many people in the way now I couldn't tell. But why would he tell lies to me? I mean he wanted to sell stuff and make a profit to feed his children surely. And there was his ora which I'd thought was good.

"Tissues," I said again. You must have them. All shops have tissues."

"No, no, no. We have no dishes in this shop. Ahmed!" He shouted through to the back shop and another man came out. I saw two people leaving the shop so it was less busy now so perhaps they didn't need the other man.

"I'm disappointed," I said. "You're not very helpful and I was just admiring your ora."

"Look please, we are busy here. If you go to the bargain stores just one street up there they have many, many dishes for you to choose in many colours and fine designs."

Oh well. I said thank you and left him to his own devices and customers. The bargain stores were on my way home anyway. But do you know when I got there the window display was full of crockery. It didn't look like a shop that would sell tissues at all. Still there was no harm in asking. I stopped by the door to blow out some of the excess stuff and it got me in a bit of a mess but I couldn't help it. I felt a bit better after that but I still had to hold my nose.

I went in the shop and there was a blonde woman standing there with her arms folded and I could tell right away that she had a problem with her ora.

"What were you doing in our doorway?" she said, in a way that I didn't like at all. I decided to ignore that question as it was probably hysterical which means it doesn't need an answer.

"I'm looking for tissues," I said.

She just stared at me so I repeated it, "Tissues."

She waved her arms about. "Of course we don't have any tissues here, this is a fine china shop. What do you think all this is?"

I thought it was a load of old tat. But I didn't say so. I know that sometimes you have to not say what you think or people get offended. It was Senga told me that and she's right of course. She's right about lots of things.

"All your dishes are very attractive, dear, and perhaps I will return later and buy some." I had to stop twice to take a breath while I said it. I decided there was no point in staying since they obviously didn't have tissues.

"Toilet paper?" I said. "That would do."

She looked at me like I had a fish growing out my forehead. "No, no toilet paper."

"Well could I use your toilet then? Just for a minute. I'll be quick." I thought that was a good idea as there must be toilet paper in their toilet.

"Please go," she said. "If you really need tissue paper the corner shop sells it. Just one street down."

I just couldn't believe it. She was telling lies, bare-cheeked lies. That was the shop I'd just come from.

"Well thank *you* very much for your *help*," I said in a very sarcaustic way.

"That's OK, now can you please go."

I was very happy to leave that place. I wouldn't be returning there to buy my cups.

It was a great relief to get back to my bit. I gave the old dripping tap a good blow and then stuffed it up again so I had both hands free. I made a cup of tea and had just sat down with it when there was this loud cheeky knock at the door. I was really very annoyed, I'd been so looking forward to a wee relax. I rushed to the door and pulled it open so quickly I bruised my knuckles on the handle.

"Ow, ow ow," I said.

There was a man standing there and he let out a kind of yelp. Well you could have blown me down with a feather 'cos it was the young postman I'd met at Senga's. He was looking like he'd just had an electrical shock from an appliance that's not had its connections checked for a long time, so I smiled to put him at his ease. He was obviously just finishing his round which was why our paths had crossed again. I took a step out the door. "You're finished now, son," I said.

"No, please, I've got a family," he screamed and he turned and ran down the stairs in a cloud of dust because it was my turn to clean them this week and I hadn't got round to it. I shut the door and went back to my cuppa. Oh well, there's some folk that you just can never understand and I'd met my fair share of them today.

Seline Gets Cultured

Have you ever been to one of them classical concerts? No, I hadn't neither, not till last week. I mean I've nothing against classy music, they have lovely tunes, like the one for Toblerone, that's a classy tune. It makes you think of mountains and chocolate and things like that, although I prefer Maltesers myself.

Anyway, like I say, it was last week and Senga, she's my best friend, said that her uncle Fergus had asked her if she would go to a concert with him, only she didn't want to go on account of he was a bit free with his hands, that's what she said, free with his hands. I didn't know what she meant so I sort of laughed and she laughed and I said ok I would go 'cos I'd never been to a classy concert. Just you keep watch on them hands of his, she said.

So there I was sat sitting in the back stalls of the Stella Hall with Fergus by me. It's a lovely place that hall. I'd never been in before. It's a bit like a baked bean tin inside, if you empty the beans out: all kind off circular with the audience where the beans would be. So then the orchestra wandered in. I thought they'd be dressed up in bow ties and black suits and all but they were all informal like they were going shopping. It said in the programme that they had a lot of guest players playing from another orchestra, like they were on their holidays. The conductor came in then and everyone clapped when he walked in so careful and didn't trip.

He picked his stick up and waved it and they started playing. Fergus told me it was a piece by Chi Cough Sky. His fifth sympathy I think it was. I liked it. It was a bit loud in places but there were lots of good tunes. It made me wish I had some Toblerone to nibble. I looked at Fergus but he had his eyes shut all carried away with the music and tapping out the rhythm with his fingers on my knee.

When it finished they pulled a big curtain across the stage and that was the end of the first half. Just one bit, you don't get much for your money, but I didn't care 'cos Fergus was paying. At the interval I told him I had to go to the toilet on account of I can't hold it in no longer on account of my operation, so he said he would get the ice creams while I done my business.

Toilets were downstairs half way along this circular corridor and after I'd washed my hands I came out and made my mistake. See, I turned the wrong way. Weren't my fault, I were thinking of the smelly hand stuff in the bathroom. There were soap to wash with and they had this creamy hand stuff to rub on your hands and keep them soft and all, which I'd done, but it made my hands all sticky and runny so I was thinking of that and just turned along the corridor and through the door at the end. I was in another corridor only this one had carpet on the floor. Half way along was a big room with double doors and a big man in front of it with arms folded. I thought he was going to tell me to hop it but when he saw me he came over all smiley and said, 'right in here, miss. Please help yourself, drinks in the corner, buffet on the table'.

It was packed with lots and lots of people all talking loud. I think some of them were from the orchestra. I pushed through the crowd and at the back was a big table all full of fancy food. It fair made my tummy grumble but no one could hear 'cos they were talking too loud. I didn't know there was free grub at classy concerts or I might have gone before. I grabbed a pastry thing and wondered if I should go and get Fergus, but I'd never be able to push through all those folk and anyways I was starving so I piled a plate and started eating. There were glasses of pink lemonade too so I grabbed a couple of them.

After a few minutes I realised this man was watching me. He looked at me and I smiled.

"Ah," he said. "A real trencherwoman, eh?"

I thought about that for a minute but it made no sense.

"Yes," I said. I find it's always best to be agreeable.

"John Embly," he said and stuck his hand out. "You must be the Bournemouth Phil."

This was very embarrassing. There was obviously something wrong with the poor man. He was talking nonsense.

"Yes," I said. "I'm Phil. Isn't it nice here."

"Well, Phyllis what's your instrument then?" he said.

"I'm the pizza," I said and reached for another slice.

He roared with laughter at that. "You're a card, Phyllis, you really are."

It was then I heard a bell ringing above the racket in the room and everyone started leaving. It wasn't long before the room was empty which suited me fine. As I say I was really sorry for the man but it's hard to make conversation when all you get back is nonsense. Oh well, might as well take advantage. I scoffed some more sausage rolls and another couple of glasses of lemonade. I couldn't believe they'd left all this food. It was then the door opened.

"For goodness sake."

There was a man standing in the doorway and he didn't look pleased, in fact he looked annoyed.

"Oh, sorry," I said. "I didn't want it to go to waste."

"Never mind that. Just hurry will you, you're going to be late."

I guessed the concert was starting. He literally pushed me out of the room.

"Will you please hurry," he said behind me as we rushed along the corridor.

"Look it's ok. I don't mind missing the start," I said. Actually I was feeling a little dizzy.

"Oh very funny. Just up the stairs and straight ahead."

"You're not very polite," I said as I climbed the stairs but he'd already turned away and was talking into his mobile.

I pushed through the door at the top and stopped. The orchestra were all sitting around with their instruments and things, blowing and bowing and hitting or whatever. Was I really supposed to be here? The man had been most insistive that I should be. Maybe it was some sort of interval thing where the orchestra entertain you with their musical knowings.

There was a spare seat at the back between the great big fiddles that they stand on the floor and the brassy people. So I sat down and watched the man beside me tune his huge thing. What a racket they make close up. I could feel all my wobblies wibble wobbling as he drew his stick across the string. He stopped and looked over at me and then sort of did a double take like you do when you can't believe Tesco are selling sausages as cheaply as that and then you put your specs on and check the expiry date and then you check your watch and you find that it's expired, the sausages expired I mean.

"Errm," he said.

I smiled at him but I thought, oh my god, not another one.

"Errm... are you..?"

"Yes," I said. "Hello, I'm Seline. Pleased to meet you I'm sure."

"Yes... right," he said and frowned down at his big giant fiddle.

"I don't know how you're going to get it under your chin," I said. It was funny because he couldn't get it under his chin. I knew that. He made a strange noise. I think he was trying to stop himself laughing. I bet no one's ever said that to him before.

Then he said, "Look, are you really supposed to be here?"

"I go where I'm told," I said.

He shook his head and waved at the leader man at the front of the orchestra. The leader stood up but right then some really bright lights came on and the big curtains at the front pulled back. Everyone in the orchestra stopped talking and the leader sat down. There was lots of applause from somewhere out the front but it was so bright from the big lights that I couldn't see a thing.

Then on came the conductor man and everyone clapped. I clapped too, and gave a whistle through my teeth. He raised his stick, looked around and smiled. Then he brought his stick down and they started playing with a big crash from the thimbles that fair made me jump out of my skin.

It felt strange being in the middle of the orchestra while they were playing. Made me wish I'd learned to play an instrumental when I was little. I'd have liked the drums. Teacher used to call me a drummy so she must have thought I was musical. Right now I was also beginning to feel a bit sick. I suppose it might have been the fizzy juice and the sausage rolls and the little sandwich things and the cheese on crackers and the pickled herring and them little cakes with the cherries and the apple pie with the drippy filling that got down my bra and the cream, or something. But I was definitely feeling cheesy-queasy.

I took a deep breath and tried to hold it in. That's what Mam always did when she felt sick which was often on a Friday night after she'd been plastering at the pub. So I sat there with my breath held, but it was no good, I could feel it gurgling around inside me and getting ready to blow. What could I do? I looked around. The man on my other side was blowing his tuba regardless of me, and there was a bin sitting beside him so I boaked in the bin and felt much better. Someone was laughing somewhere but it weren't on the stage. I don't think none of them had noticed.

And then, my God, pardon me for the language, but the tuba man stopped blowing and picked up the waste bin.

"No," I said and tried to grab it from him.

"Hey... what..? Let go. Who the four asterisks are you?" he hissed at me.

Actually he didn't say 'four asterisks' instead he used a very bad word which I don't like and which you hear sometimes in the chip shop when the chippy man dips his thing in the fryer. You may know it begins with an F and ends with a K and has a number of other letters in between. So I let go of the bucket and, blow me if he didn't stick it in the end of his tuba.

There was going to be an embarrassment, I just knew it. I looked around but no one was watching me, except the conductor man, who had a very funny look on his face. I got up with extreme quietness and backed away towards the door.

I stood outside for a minute. This had all been very strange. Then the orchestra started playing very loud, and then there was screams and shouts and they all stopped. I could hear laughing too. I backed away from the door as the shouting got louder and ran downstairs and along the corridor. I stopped at the foody place and had a quick look inside. It was all still there so I filled my handbag before trotting along the corridor. All the audience were leaving. Some of them were laughing fit to bust a gut but some didn't look pleased at all

Oh well, not everyone likes classy music.

Seline the Artist

Art's important you know. People have been doing it for years, art I mean. I like the old stuff, all them old masters and mistresses. Those sunflowers and Rembrandt, he's good, but I like all the new stuff too. It's all new and doesn't need cleaning as much as the old stuff. Have you seen yon Mr. Triano's paintings? He's good. You know, the one who does the umbrellas and the ladies in their pants with funny eyes? He's a Vet, 'though you wouldn't think it to look at him. I saw him in the queue in Sainsbury yesterday. Recognised him right away. He didn't recognise me, of course. I mean I've not been on telly or anything, although Senga did say she saw me in the audience on Parkinson once. She swore it was me although I can't remember being there. Mind my memories nor what it was. Anyway I said to this guy. "You're that Triano fella, aren't you?"

I didn't like the look he gave me. Viscous it was. You don't see that look when he's on the telly. "What?" he says.

"Triano, the arty-farty fella. I know you."

"I don't know what you're talking about," he says and goes back to unloading his cabbages.

Well that was a bit cheeky, I thought. I mean he only had to be civil. I wasn't going to ask him for an opinion on my artworks or anything. And then he dropped his last cabbage and I grabbed it.

"I believe this is yours," I said, and handed it back. What does anyone need with four cabbages? Perhaps he was going to paint them or feed his animals.

"Would you like to look at these drawings," I said.

"Oh please," he said which was rather nice of him. After all he's famous. but I looked down to get them out of my handbag, looked up, and he was gone. Vanished.

"Where'd he go?" I said to the checkout girl.

She shrugged. "Can I help you pack," she said, as if I was going on holiday or something.

"Not until the summer," I said.

I left her packing and went out to the front but he wasn't there. Oh well, Seline, I thought. That could have been you're big chance.

It was then I saw the advert for the exhibition. *Artist's Now* it said and *all welcome* which was rather nice of them. I thought I'd take my paintings along and hang them up.

I had tea and then I remembered it was bin day and I'd forgotten to put the bin out again. All this week's rubbish and last week's was sitting there. Then I thought, well, the gallery has a huge rubbish bin down the side. I could take a bag and dump it and see all the arty stuff at the same time. Killing two birds with one whatsit so to speak.

So there I was outside the gallery with my black bin bag only there wasn't any bin. They must have taken it away. They're everywhere these days. Oh well, I thought, might as well look at the paintings. I wandered into the gallery. There was a fat man just inside the door.

"Excuse me," he said all polite like.

"Of course," I said.

"Can I look in your bag?" he said.

Well I know people get to like all sorts, but a bag of rubbish? Then I remembered Senga had told me about a programme on the telly with all these people sitting around talking about what, you know, turns them on. Quite disgusting she said it was. She recorded it for me.

"You a perv?" I said.

"Actually I'm Ahmed," he said. "I must look in your bag."

"Well, OK," I said "But it's just rubbish."

He pulled open the top of the bag and stuck his hand inside. He got a funny look on his face. "Cheese us," he said or something like it and pulled his hand out sharpish. I thought that was rather strange. I never have cheese in the house.

"You can't bring that in here," he shouted. He was holding one hand out in front of him and searching for something with the other. "I'm gonna wash this off. You wait there and don't move." He looked quite upset, poor luv.

"Can I leave it here?" I said.

"No you can't. Just... just... wait that's all." And he was off through a door at the back. Talk about weird. It's difficult to understand some people. Perhaps he was the cleaner.

Well I thought I might as well take a quick peek while I was waiting so I swung my bag over my shoulder and went through the swing doors into the gallery. It was a huge room but there didn't seem to be much on show. There was a big glass case with fish swimming round and a fishing rod sticking out with the hook dangling outside. *Gone Fishin'* the label said and then there was a cassette recorder with a picture of Dracula behind it, *scream saver* that one was called and then there was the toilet.

It was sitting in the middle of the room, a toilet cubicle, three sides and a door that said *gentlemen*. There was a big grey cylinder round the back. Just for a moment I thought it was real, but then I thought there's never going to be a single cubicle right in the middle of the gallery now is there? I mean that's just silly. Go on have a look I told myself and yet I didn't like to. It said gentlemen after all, I mean who knew what might be in there. I touched the brass handle and ran my fingers over the door. It was real wood. A lovely piece of oak all polished and everything. I've always liked a nice piece of wood. Uncle Bernie used to have a wooden leg. He lost it in the war, Mam said, so that's why they had to give him a metal one.

"Watch out for Uncle Bernie, Seline," she said. "He may be short of a leg but he's not short in the other department." I don't know what she meant. He wasn't any taller than me.

Oh well, I gave the door a shove and it opened. All that was inside was a toilet bowl with a fancy blue lid and a cistern with a chain. And then there was a funny noise, a rude noise like, you know and the water in the bowl went all bubbly and frothy. I lifted the lid up and bent over to have a closer look. I'd just worked out that it was the gas cylinder round the back causing the water to bubble when the bag I had slung over my shoulder came right over my head and walloped into the bowl. Of course the bag split open and all the rubbish was everywhere.

Half of it was down the toilet and the rest over the floor. Just as well there was no-one else in the gallery. I stuffed some more down the toilet and then sat down beside the heap to think. Perhaps I could put some in the fish tank? Then this man in a suit burst into the room. He had a bow tie and a carnation in his buttonhole. I think he was going to a wedding. He stood staring at me.

"Wonderful," he said. "It's beautiful. I'm overwhelmed."

Then he said, "Are you the artist?" and I understood.

"I could show you," I said. I'd still got my drawings with me.

"It's too much," he said.

"There's only a few of them," I said.

"The artist surrounded by her art. It's a magnificent sight. What do you call it? Ah here it is. 'Bog oak'. That's just magnificent. It's so right. It explains everything."

"It does?" I said.

"The used tissues and the texture of the wood, the empty cans and bin liner and the plum stone. The juxtaposition of organic and inorganic with the spiritual overtones. It's so..."

"Smelly?" I said.

"Yes, yes. It must have been difficult to balance the olfactory experience."

"Well actually I overbalanced." I said.

There was a funny gurgling noise from the toilet bowl. I had a sudden horrible thought.

"Have you exhibited before?"

"Certainly not. I'm from Musselborough. Mam never allowed it."
The cheek of him.

"First time, eh? Well, well. The virgin artist, what?" He was grinning all over his fat face.

"I had a boyfriend... once."

"Ah haven't we all," he pipes up all wistful like.

"He emigrated."

"Foolish boy. If only he could see you now eh? Your own exhibition."

Brian wasn't interested in exhibitions. He worked in the fish shop. Said he'd take me out. We went to McDonalds. He stank of fish. We both had burgers and he took me home. He tried some funny business, said he'd like me to fry his haddock but I battered his plaice instead.

"Well..."

"Look, to business. My card." He gave me a white card 'Ffrancis S. Duchamp FRAA' it said in gold letters. It didn't say where he was frae though.

"On the strength of what I've seen I'm prepared to offer you a commission for my new gallery."

"I'm not paying," I said.

"No, no my dear lady. I will pay you for the art work you produce."

"I've got a few drawings."

"No, no. I need action pieces like this." He pointed at the remains of my binbag.

"The council don't pay me anything."

"Council. Pah. The arts council wouldn't recognise talent if it bit them on the bum. Just let me know when you're ready."

I couldn't believe what he was saying. "You want me to bring my stuff to your gallery."

"When you're ready."

"All of it?"

"The more the better, dear lady. Just tell me how much space you need."

"I could bring them round this afternoon."

"Wonderful, marvellous. I shall be intrigued."

The toilet made another strangulated gurgle.

"Could you just look at these," I said pulling out my drawings.

"Oh never mind that rubbish," he says. "Just concentrate on the installation."

Rubbish! Rubbish? I'd spent hours doing those sketches. And here he was calling them rubbish and he hadn't even looked at them. I'll give you rubbish I thought.

"You'll need to wait," I said. "It's not finished."

"Fascinating," he said.

There was a hissing juddering noise from the cubicle like something was trying to escape. "Just wait in here," I said. "It'll be a surprise."

He rubbed his hands together and stood inside the cubicle. There was a rumbling noise like thunder. I reversed quickly towards the exit and slipped through the door.

"Oi. you!" It was the strange cleaner man. He was advancing towards me with an odd look on his face. "I told you to wait."

"Well excuse me," I said "You're talking to an artist."

His reply was lost in the explosion. He stared at me, mouth hanging open, and then rushed through to the gallery with a shout of, "Wait there."

I reckoned I'd better not. So I headed outside.

I don't suppose he'll want my exhibit now, I thought, as the ambulance wailed round the corner. But perhaps I'd take my bin bags round to his gallery anyway.

Seline at the Bank

I decided to go down the bank. It's not that I was worried, I mean I know my banks safe as it's been in the high street for years not like those banks that haven't and just disappear as soon as you stop watching them. I've got a lot of money in the bank see. Mam's pension goes in there now that she's gone and I don't touch it so it cumulates and gets loads of interest. That means it's worth more than it was last year. I must have hundreds of pounds in there now which I'm saving up for my dotage. That's where Senga my friend says I'll be soon.

Anyway what with all the bank problems these days I took the bus into town at 2.26pm. I got off in the high street. It was all humbly-tumbly with people all rushing about with bags and stuff. And they're all so young these days, in my days it was only old people went shopping

It was confusing. Sometimes I get confused when too much is happening and I have to sit right down and have a cup of tea.

A lady stopped me in the high street with a clip board. "Are you happy," she said.

I thought it was a bit personal but she had a nice smile and looked all official with her clippyboard and all. "Oh yes, thank you," I said. "I'm very happy, thank you. I hope you are too. I'd be even happier if I could get a cup of tea."

"Ah you're a tea drinker," she said and she made a note on her clipboard.

"Yes," I said. "I just told you."

"So can you tell me what kind of tea you drink?"

I had to think carefully about that, see Senga usually buys the tea, as the last time I bought it she says I came back with cocoa.

"Tea bags," I said. "You know the things with perforations that let all the flavour out."

She'd been going to write something down but she closed her eyes instead.

"And Senga doesn't like cocoa."

"She doesn't like..."

"Cocoa, but I think it's fine. Do you like it?"

"What?"

"I said do you like cocoa." I'd decided she must be a bit deaf so I spoke louder so she could hear me.

She moved a step backwards. "I've never had it."

"You've never had cocoa?" I said

"No... no, I don't think so and can you please stop shouting."

She was fiddling so much with her pen that she dropped it. I bent down to pick it up and she screamed. Just a little high pitched scream like a door makes when you don't oil it.

"Just like a door," I said.

"What?" Her mouth was hanging open in a most uncomplimentary way. She had confused me so I didn't know whether to raise or lower my voice now. I tried to be somewhere in the middle.

"You should keep your mouth shut." I said. "It's more ladylike. My Mam was always telling me to keep my mouth shut."

She took three steps backwards. "Look, sorry for bothering you. I've got to go now. Things... you know."

"Yes, yes of course, peace and love," I said and I raised my two fingers in the gesture for peace. I saw someone do that on the news the other day.

"Holy shit," said the woman and walked away, although she kept looking over her shoulder and so bumped into a piece of street furniture and fell over.

I was going to help her but many people gathered around her and would be able to render assistance to the poor woman. She was saying something and several people looked over at me, so I thought I'd better be getting on to the bank.

It's a big building with pillars outside at the end of the high street. I remembered from when I was last there, years ago. There was a man in a suit standing just inside the door.

"Can I help you?" he said, all friendly and helpful like.

"Yes, thank you, I hope you can. I have an account see."

"You want to check it over to see how much you..."

"Yes, that's right dear. Just to see how much I have."

He took me over to a big desk all cluttered with papers and such, and sat down. Up behind him were a whole lot of big rolls of carpet. I guess they were getting themselves made over. I've watched programmes about it.

"Everybody's at it these days," I said.

"At it," he said. "Well yes, I suppose."

"I hope you're not using my money for it then."

He went a bit red in the face. "I'm not quite sure..."

"For all this carpet."

He looked around. "Well, yes we are of course."

"Anyone would think this was a carpet shop."

He stared at me and then he grinned and then he coughed and then he frowned.

"Well... yes this is a carpet shop."

Now I hadn't expected him to say that. He was making a joke of course so I laughed to make him feel happy. You want to keep your bank happy. "Get away," I said and clapped him on the shoulder.

"Ow," he said and then "Ah Christ," and rubbed his shoulder as if I'd hurt him. I mean to say, I'd only tapped him in a friendly gesture of mutual jokiness and good humourous and there he was making a dog's mess of it. Mind you the postman says I'm quite strong.

He stood up and said all snappy like. "You'll have to leave. I can't have this."

I wasn't having it either. "You can't do that. I came here to talk about my bank account. I am very unhappy with your customer service skills. I demand to see the manager.

"Glory be," he put both hands on his head which made him look like a jug with a handle at both sides. "This isn't a bank. I told you, this is 'Rug-4u'. We're a carpet shop.

"But I used to come here..."

"Yes it *used* to be a bank but that was ten years ago. They moved round the corner, Sydney street. They couldn't afford the rent here."

Ten years? Surely it wasn't as long ago as that. "If you're making this up to get rid of me I'll not be pleased. I'll have you know I've got a big account."

He was breathing very hard through his nose, sounded a bit like an old steam engine. I'd been looking round the walls and you know there were rather a lot of carpet rolls and they had prices on too. Oh well. I stood up and put my hand out.

"Pleased to meet you," I said.

"Just go," he said.

"You're a very rude young man," I said. "I wouldn't put my money here even if you were a bank.

"Christ almighty, just go will you?"

"I certainly will and I will not be recommending your carpets. I believe they are very likely to be of poorer quality than those available elsewhere and you should not blaspheme like that."

He looked quite distracted now. "You're mad and I'm not blanking blaspheming."

Actually, where I said blanking, he used a word that I've heard quite a lot on channel four lately. I asked Senga about it last week 'cos I wasn't sure what it meant. She took a long time to answer and then she told me to think about what Benny had done when he took me round behind the toilets after school, and she gave a big wink. That's what it means she said. So I guess it's something to do with smoking and of course we all know how bad smoking is for us, don't we?

The man was jumping up and down now like a seagull looking for worms. "You can be assured that I shall not return to your smoking shop I said," and I marched towards the door.

"What?" he said as I reached the door.

I looked back and saw him kind of collapse into his chair. "What?" I heard him say again as I pulled the door open. I tried to slam it shut behind me to show him how very not pleased I was with him but it had one of those springy thingys on it so it didn't.

Well, what with that man and his smoking carpets and his bad civility I was quite put upon and didn't feel like going around the corner to the bank, so I took the bus home and Senga made me a nice cup of tea and a dooky biscuit and listened to my story. I felt much better after that. She suggested I go to the real bank next time and try and buy a carpet but I thought that was a silly idea and I told her so.

Seline's Family Tree

"Can I help you?" said the nice man at the bookshop door with the green tie.

I gave him my soaking umbrella to hold while I carried on looking at the magazines.

I had just popped into the book shop to get out of the rain, so that's why I was stood standing at the magazines. I wasn't going to buy anything, I mean they're all so expensive - pounds they cost, most of them. I remember when you could get the People's Friend for 6d, mind I couldn't afford it then either. You can buy magazines on anything these days. Senga, she's my best friend, bought one the other day that was just about a field in Scotland. I don't know how you can write a magazine about a field. Anyway I had a look through one or two just so I wouldn't look too odd while I was waiting for the rain to go off.

I picked up *Gay Gardener* because I like flowers and gardening and stuff like that but it was a little strange.

"Excuse me." It was the man with the green tie. He was looking embarrassed. "I think this is your umbrella," he said.

I took a close look at it. "Yes, that's mine," I said. It's quite easy to tell on account of it's purple with a lion on and a broken spoke.

"I think you should take it back," he said.

"Yes of course," I said. "I'll get it just as soon as I leave. You just wait over by the door."

I put the *Gay Gardener* back, I didn't understand it. It was then I saw the magazine beside it - *Gentle Genealogy vol1 no1* it called itself, and underneath *Genealogy for the fainthearted*. Actually, at first I thought it said farted rather than fainthearted. You know how sometimes you read words that aren't really there, it can be quite embarrassing. I had to read it several times. I think fainthearted made more sense. I knew what Genealogy was, I saw a programme on telly about it, and it just suddenly came to me what Mam used to say about our family, only I've forgot what it was right now, but anyway when she said it I remember thinking that surely they couldn't have been as bad as that.

I started reading the introduction in the magazine and it told about how easy it was to find out about all your famous ancestors. I got to thinking how I might be related to the Queen or even that Barbara Dickson with the voice.

"Excuse *me*." It was that man with the silly tie. He was waving my umbrella around and looking quite agitated. He was obviously not right in the head. "I am not an umbrella stand," he says.

I stared at him. Well what can you say? I mean he looked perfectly normal. I didn't want to antagonise him, him not having quite enough fat in the pan, as Mam used to say.

"No, no indeed you're not," I said. I smiled at him to try and make him feel relaxed but it didn't work. His face went quite red. Normally I would have given him a talk about customer service but this was not the moment.

"Look, I'm just going to buy this magazine right over here by the door where that nice lady takes the money. Then I'll collect my umbrella from you, even though you are not an umbrella stand, and you can go back to being whatever you are, which will be nice now, won't it?"

His eyes had gone all bulgy and his nostrils were flared out like he was breathing really, really hard. He didn't say anything more but marched over to the door holding my umbrella between his finger tips. A tall man in a bow tie talked to him. He waved his arms about but then he seemed to calm down after that.

I joined the queue to pay for my magazine. The tie man was standing near the door with his eyes shut, sort of rocking backwards and forwards gently and I realised that he really looked sort of, you know... nice. He was a wee bit taller than me and maybe a bit older but he had all his hair and looked very smart in his shiny shoes. OK perhaps he was a bit short upstairs but at least he could tie his shoelaces. Right, Seline, I thought, use your willies. That's what Mam used to tell me, if you want to get your man, Seline, you've got to use your feminine willies. I tipped my hat slightly sideways and undid the top button of my raincoat. It didn't seem much so I undid another button and pulled out the collar of my cardie. Well it would have to do for the moment. The lady behind the till was staring at me peculiarly.

"It's not for you, dear," I said and gave her a big wink. I think she got the message, she served me really quickly.

I sauntered over to the man by the door, who still seemed to have his eyes shut. I stood beside him for a second and then I leant over and said in his ear. "You can give it me now. I'm ready."

He jumped backwards and let out this funny sort of gurgling noise and dropped my brolly right at my feet which really was a bit silly considering he'd been holding it all this time. He was lying back against the wall with his hand on his chest just sort of staring at me and making these strange noises. He really was a most peculiar man, too peculiar for me, I decided. I picked up my brolly, thanked him and left.

The rain had stopped so I decided to walk home. An ambulance came screeching round the corner a few minutes later making an awful racket.

I told Senga about it when I got home. "Trust you to fall for an umbrella stand, love," was all she said. I don't think she quite understood what I was saying

"What do you think about genealogy, Senga," I said.

"If it keeps you out of mischief, Seline, I'm all for it," she said.

Seline's Alien Encounter

MEMO

From: Xan X Blong, Deep spaceexplorer 9, Elanger
system
To: Commanders office

Re: Routine investigation

Location   Elanger system. Planet 3 (only planet with
sentient life.)
Subject   Typical Biped
Height   1.7 M (local units)
Mass   55Kg (local units)
Sex   Indeterminate (see report)

Report from field agents:
Subject was sedated and removed from habitation module.
Installation in quarters was problematic as we had been misinformed
re species median volume (please update local manual).
On recovery, subject was extracted from quarters and examined.
Appeared to be undamaged although emitting much noise from
vocalisation orifice. Translation module inadequately programmed
for this species although after some discussion with observation
committee there was agreement that subjects principal phonation
related to primitive anger emotion. Sexual assignment was not
possible due to lack of examinational opportunities.

It would appear there is a possibility that....

Report Ends

"Look, I told you a dozen times, they were blue, blue."
"Yes, but please calm down, Miss Allbright. It's important for us to know exactly what happened. I'd really like you to explain right from the beginning."
"But they probed me, you know?"
"Yes, you mentioned. Now, please, from the start."
"Well, all right. But they need to be arrested, going around probing all and sundry. It was awful. It's not decent. I'll bet you've never been probed."
"Please."
"Well, it was Thursday, see. That's my washing day, always has been. I was hanging it out on the line. It was after midnight so it was real dark but I had Uncle Bill's torch, you know the one with the red knob on the end for signalling to boy scouts? I balanced it on the coal bunker, so I could see. I didn't want anyone to see me, see 'cos I got this snotty nose with the cold and I had toilet paper stuck up my nostrils. Anyway, I was just pegging out my pink vest when I heard this buzzing noise like there's a hive of bees or wasps or other winged stingy things. I thought of them killer bees right away, so I stuck my pants over my head. But the noise just got louder and louder until I thought, them's not bees. So I peeked out my pants and there's this shimmering sparkly light all shimmering and sparking and these two blue things materialised right in front of me. Frightening it was."
"Can you describe these blue things, Miss Allbright."
"Well, they weren't very big like, no bigger than Senga really and she's not tall. She's big other ways of course, I mean round the way you know, but she's not tall and neither were they. But they had all

these blue things waving about. Like tentacles I suppose, but not as long as tentacles. I mean not like an octopus tentacles, not with suckers. More sort off suggestible like if you know what I mean. I mean you're a man ain't you? You should know. Anyway I tried not to look but it was sort of difficult on account of they were waving them in my face. Look, are you writing this down?"

"Of course, Miss Allbright. Every word. So what happened then?"

"Well, one of them got behind me and pushed me towards the sparkly thing. I knew it was a ship of course, I mean I've read about these things in the News of the World. I knew that resistance was futile, they must have put that into my mind see, 'cos that's all I could think off - resistance is futile - resistance is..."

"Miss Allbright?"

"Yes, ok, I'm only telling you, right? So anyway, there was no point in resisting as it would have been futile, so I let him push me and a door opened in the side of the sparkly thing and he shoved me right inside."

"And what was it like inside this... sparkly thing, Miss Allbright?"

"Well, it was all sort of bright and shiny and dazzly, so dazzly I had to shut my eyes until they adjusted to the dazlingness. I was fair nauseated with it all. The two blue things pushed in behind me and there wasn't a lot of room, I mean it wasn't like your Tardis sort of thing where it's bigger on the outside than it is in the middle. No, sorry, I mean the other way. So these things with their tentacles were all pressed up against me. I didn't bend over I can tell you. I'm a respectable woman I'll have you know and I hope you're writing that down. I was brought up right to mind my qs and ps."

"And then?"

"Well then, there I was and there they were, so they push me into this tiny plastic box thing and try to close the lid only they couldn't on account of it was too small, the box, not the lid, so one of them started pushing and prodding me and trying to squash me in. Well I wasn't having any of that. I just told him - You can't treat me like this - I said. - I pay my taxes. And I gave him a dunt on one of his tentacles. Well, he started squealing like I don't know what. Actually, I remember, it sounded a bit like Dad when Mam caught his pants in the ringer, he still had then on see. That's why I say you have to be careful when you bend over, you never know what's coming. It's a bit like when I went to get money from the bank with my card thing and their stupid machine exploded. It weren't none of my fault before you say anything."

"I wasn't going to say anything, Miss Allbright."

"Were so. I could see it in your eyes. You were going to say I done it, just like the bank man... and the police... and the social... and Senga. But they'd let it go rusty. You could see the rust inside when it fell apart. Stupid thing was probably made in China by some poor little lassie trying to keep her mother in sarongs for peanuts."

"Please, Miss Allbright... please."

"Are you all right, son? You look a bit peeky. You should get more fresh air. Go to the seaside. It's the ozone there you know - good for you."

"Miss Allbright..."

"Oh yes, sorry. Well, there I was in the box and there's this alien jumping up and down and holding his tentacle and making this awful din. It was then, they done it."

"Done what... did what?

"Well, you know, probed me. This thing came down from the ceiling and before you could say flutter by butterfly they'd invaded all my privacys. Well, they didn't stay there long I can tell you. No sir. I just lost it."

"Lost... it?"

"Yes, I lost it, my temper. I don't loose my temper often you know. Well, you don't know I suppose, but it's true. You just ask anyone and they'll tell you, Seline is a model of non-temper lossiness they'll say. But these alien guys had just pushed me too far. I mean you just don't do that sort of thing in our country. I think I must have screamed and shouted a bit, maybe threw my arms around too because they kind of jumped back smartish and made kind of wobbly noises, you know like a jelly might make if it could make noises. That's when I managed to squeeze out of the box. And I gave them another earful. I told them it was just ridiculous and that I was going to write to my MP once I found who he was and stuff like that. That's when I noticed."

"Noticed? Noticed what, Miss Allbright?"

"That they were looking a bit sort of... not well. I mean, I didn't know what they should look normally, but they just looked odd. One of them was kind off bouncing off the wall and their tentacles had all gone limp. Anyway they threw me out."

"Just threw you out?"

"Yup, just like that, as Tommy Cooper used to say. Do you remember him? No, you're too young. He had a fez with a tassle. Anyway they left me all of a heap in the middle of the green, with my washing all wrapped round me. I had to do the whole lot again. Bleedin' ridiculous, pardon me, but really, I ask you. Would you like a drink? No, I suppose you can't, not on duty. Well, you just send that report to the high-up yins, son. Make sure something gets done about it. I blame the Russians myself, they've probably made an agreablement with the aliens to do stuff... and things... whatever. Oh, are you off? Well, shut the gate on your way out, there's a good lad."

NEWS OF THE ENGELBLAAT

Yesterday Xan X Blong and Tet X Ringar, senior officers, Deep spaceexplorer 9 were buried with full honours on their ship's early return, under auto-pilot, from the Elanger system. Both officers were infected by a virulent plague contracted from an experimental subject. Our thoughts are with their families at this difficult time. A quarantine has been placed on the entire system.

Seline's Holiday

"I've decided to take a holiday. Everyone's doing it, even yon woman that reads the news, what's her face, the one with the fluttery eyes. She said she was taking a holiday right after the weather. I haven't had a holiday for a long time, not since... when was decimalisation? Oh never mind I can't remember either. It was a waste of time, all those new pennies and pounds and stuff, now it's Euros and where's that got us eh?"

"So where would you like to go exactly, Miss Allbright?"

I jumped. I mean really jumped. I'd quite forgotten where I was. It happens sometimes when I'm talking to people. I get carried away. The young man had been so quiet, hardly a squeak, in fact he seemed to be in a bit of a daze. He was the travel agent, at least he was sitting behind a desk when I came into the shop. There were three of them, all looking bored. I was just looking for some brochures really, for ideas. He asked if he could help me. The other two ladies didn't even look at me, one of them shook her head at him. My feet were so sore and he looked really nice so I sat down.

"I'd like somewhere hot, somewhere dry. Can't stand the rain in this stupid country. I need to get away from the rain. It's all acid you know, rots the brain, that's why I wear a hat, see." I pointed at my hat. "What's your name?"

"Um, Norman. It's nice." It was. I think Norman's a lovely name. His voice was all husky and he stared at my hat with big round eyes. He really was a most attractive young man. I was beginning to feel all woozy. I knew if I stood up my knees would be shaking. Mam had warned me about men like him. The woozers she called them. Watch out for the woozers Seline. Don't ever say you will. Keep them dancing. Keep it plutonic. I think she was talking about yon sex stuff. But I could never be bothered myself, too messy and all that huffing and puffing, what's the point? I saw it in yon dancing film, Last Tango in Paris. I fell asleep and must have missed the dancing but there was plenty of huffing.

"Are you a dancer, Norman?"

"What? No...not really."

"Good, very sensible. Keep it that way."

He stared at me for ages with those brown eyes. I stared back. His eye lashes were really long. I could get lost in those eyes.

Finally I broke the trance. Someone had to. "What were we talking about," I said.

"Y... y... your holiday," he said. He seemed to have developed a bit of a stammer. I gave him my nicest smile to put him at his ease. He was very young after all. His eyebrows shot up.

"Are you all right?" he said.

"Me? Never felt better."

"Sorry, it's just you look as if something's hurting you."

"No, no. I'm fine. Just a bit woozy though, you know." I gave him a big wink just in case that was too subtle. He took a deep breath. He got the message all right. Trying to control his passionate feelings. The girl on his right was reading a book now.

"Miss Allbright. You want to go somewhere hot for a holiday. Can I recommend the Balearics."

"As long as they're nowhere near Worcester. Don't like Worcester. Me Mam got stuck in a traffic jam in Worcester. Sharing a cab with my Dad she was. That's where I was deceived she said. Well I don't like people lying to me. It's not nice. So I've never gone to Worcester, mind it doesn't stop them lying, they do it all the time. Council are the worst. Are you all right?"

The poor boy had gone all red.

"Fine," he said. He was wheezing a bit like he'd got asthma. Cats can bring it on.

"You got a cat, then?"

"No, no animals at all. Look please..."

I looked at him. He was so handsome. I think I must have sighed out loud.

"The Balearics are nowhere near Worcester. They're in Spain."

"Ah, that's hot then."

"Yes, normally it is. When would you like to go?" He looked a little more relaxed.

"Well, I thought maybe around my birthday."

"Great. When's that then?" He sounded really enthusiastic.

"My birthday? Well that's 22nd of June."

"Fantastic. That's a great time to go to Spain. I'm sure I can find you something."

He turned to his computer and started pressing buttons.

"I've got one of them."

"Have you now?"

"Yes, my neighbour had one as well. Well actually he had lots. He was a strange man. I never did figure what he was up to. Anyway you've got to have one these days, that's what Senga says. Senga, she's my friend. We meet for coffee every day, except Tuesday, I go to the library on Tuesday and Wednesday that's when I go to the bank, just to take some money out but it seems to take such a long time. They're not very efficient in spite of their computers and mobiles and stuff and the manager can be very rude. He's got no idea of customer service. Senga says I should go somewhere else but I don't know. What did you say?"

"Oh nothing, nothing. I've just done this wrong. Can't seem to concentrate."

"It's modern life what does it. That's what Senga says. Always so much to do. Everyone rushing about like they've got ants in their knickers. We all need to slow down. 'What is life if when we're there, we haven't time to stand the fare' or something like that. It's a poem. I read it in a book from the library. Anyway...what was I saying? Oh yes. Senga's got a blue one."

"She must be cold then."

I looked at him. He had a funny expression on his face.

"Cold?"

"Yeah cold like in blue with cold." He made a funny noise in his throat. It could have been a touch of bronchitis. We sat quiet for ages.

Finally I said. "Well OK then, but I got a yellow one. It goes with the suite. The man from the computer shop set it up for me. Said he'd be back, but he never came, anyway it's working fine. Makes a lovely hum, bit like yours."

He smiled. "Do you use it then or just listen to it?"

Listen to it? Now what would be the point of listening to your computer? I began to think Norman had a bit too much hay in the loft.

"Oh, I use it all right. There's loads of stuff I do on it. Important stuff *you* know." I gave him a wink just to make sure he got the message. Mind you I wasn't going to tell him. There's some things you've got to keep quiet about. If word got out *they* might hear. You can't trust anyone. That's what Senga says.

"You're not one of... them are you?" I thought I might as well come out with it.

He looked like someone had poked him with a live wire. "No, no absolutely not. Whatever made you say that? I'm a married man." His face was bright red again. There was a spluttering from the girl at the next desk. I think her coffee had gone down the wrong way. So he was married. Oh well, Seline, another chance gone. Or was it? It didn't really matter these days did it? People had affairs without even thinking about it. The papers were full of it. Senga's neighbour had an affair on the Internet. She told me all about it.

Norman was talking to himself.

"What did you say?" I asked him.

"I was saying we must get our business finished. The shop shuts in three hours."

"Three hours now eh." Why did people always rush so? "Have you got an e-mail address."

81

"Yes of course. It's on our notepaper. Here take a sheet."

"I really meant your address Norman." I let my hand just sort of skiff along his. "So that I can contact *you*, you know."

"You can contact me through the shop." The poor boy's voice was quivering, with anticipation I suppose. Oh well it would have to do.

"That's fine then, Norman." I stood up.

"But Miss Allbright, your holiday?"

"I thought you were organising that?"

"Yes but... but we need to... you know."

"OK then." I sat down again.

"Look, there's something here." He was tapping away at the keyboard. He sounded desperate. Poor lad, he probably needed the commission. "Two weeks in Majorca, starting 22nd of June, half board £515. How does that sound?"

"Beautiful." His voice was really very melodious. He would have made a great newsreader.

"Great." He made a fist. "I'll print off the details. As it's very close. I'll need to get 50% now. I hope that's all right?"

I looked at him. "Very close? How do you mean?"

"Well it's only two months away."

"I don't understand you Norman. It's two years away yet."

"Two years?" His voice had gone very high pitched.

"Yes, 2006 I'm going. That's when my birthday is."

"But..."

"My special birthday, you know. But I'm not telling you how special, nosy."

"You're not taking a holiday 'till 2006? You mean I've spent..." He looked at his watch. He looked at me. He looked to either side. He looked like he was shrinking.

"That's right. You can print the details." His eyes were glazed. His hand was trembling. "That will be all right won't it? I mean we could start again."

"No! I mean no, sorry I didn't mean to shout. Sorry. How many people? One I suppose."

I thought for a minute. "No, for two. I'll book for two. A *double* room please."

Outside I let my mind wander over the pleasant prospect of a holiday. Two years. Yes, plenty of time to develop our friendship. I was sure we had lots in common. Norman, you are a lucky boy.

Seline's Hobby

I've always enjoyed writing. I always got top marks for it at school. Mostly Es, sometimes Ds when I had an off day.

"I'm sure we all wish we could write like you, Seline," my teacher used to say. Made me really proud.

I stopped after I left school because I was too busy looking after Mam. She was quite old so she needed a lot of looking after. It was so sad when she left us. One minute there she was sitting in her usual chair smoking her pipe.

"I'm just off down the shops for a slice of Emmental," I said, and she just sort of nodded and waved at me. I just love cheese, especially the kind with big holes. Senga, she's my friend, says you can taste the holes. We had a tasting session once. We got all these different kinds of cheese; blue, orange, pink, green and sat and ate them while we watched Parkie. I got a bit sick. Anyway when I got back from the shops there she was, gone. I searched the house but there was no sign of her. Senga helped me search round about. We tried the pub and the Legion and the PDSA but no, she'd really gone.

It was a month later I got the postcard. *Sorry luv, couldn't take any more, having a lovely time etc.* that's all it said. It was from Paris or Panama or one of those places. It began with a 'P' or maybe it was Amsterdam, anyway it meant I'd no-one to look after so I needed something to fill up the time. I took up writing again. I mean I was good at it and lots of people publish books these days, so I thought I would too.

There was an advert for a writers' circle in our local paper. Actually it was for a Wirters' Circle but I guessed what they meant. I thought I might be able to help them so I went along on Tuesday night.

They met at the community centre. "Can you tell me where the writers' thing meets," I said to the man at the desk.

"Writers, hah," he said. He wrinkled his nose up like there was a bad smell. That wasn't a very good start.

"Yes, can you tell me where they meet?"

"Right lot of loonies if you ask me."

I was going to say that I hadn't, but he looked rather cross.

"I just want to know what room they're in. I want to join."

"It's room twelve top of the stairs but you'd be better doing tapestry in thirteen."

"Thank you but I'm a writer you see. I don't do tapestry."

"You're on your own luv, just watch out for that dragon that takes the class. Bite your head right off she would."

I think that's what we call a figure of speech. He's not really saying she's a dragon, not with fire and so on. Just that she looks like a dragon without the scales and the big mouth.

"Thank you for your time," I said

"Watch you're back, luv," he said. "Not that it's no skin of my nose."

I climbed the steps and found room twelve at the top. There was frosted glass in the door and I could see there were people inside.

I knocked and went in. They all stopped talking and stared at me. There were ten of them sitting round a big square of tables. There was a woman at the top.

"Hello," I said. "You must be the dragon. I've come to join. I thought you might need help. I'm a writer see."

She just sat there staring at me. "It's Seline. Seline Allbright. You may have heard of me. I was in the Courier last week. They interviewed me about that silly accident in Tesco. They shouldn't keep things on the top shelf."

A couple of the class laughed. She glared at them and they stopped. I put my hand out and she shook it.

"Amy, Amy Walters is the name. Welcome to our little group, Seline. Just have a seat and join in when you want."

There was only one empty seat so I sat between two men.

"Hello, I'm Seline," I said to the one on my right. He was an old man with grey hair.

"John," he said and shook my hand.

"Hello, I'm Seline," I said to the one on my left. He had long black hair and a beard.

Amyamy coughed. "Seline, we try not to have conversations among ourselves."

I searched in my pocket until I found it then I threw it across the table to her.

"It's a barley sugar," I said. "It'll help your cough. Sorry it's a bit fluffy."

She coughed again but she never tried it. Some people are so ungrateful.

"We were just listening to some poems, Seline. We bring a piece of work along each week for discussion, but don't worry you don't have to do anything this week.

"I've got a poem," I said. "In fact I've got dozens. I'll read you one if you like."

She looked round the table as if she was expecting someone to say something but nobody did.

"Well, all right, let's hear your poem, Seline." She didn't sound very enthusiastic. I don't suppose she hears many good poets.

I felt in my handbag for the paper I'd brought with me. It was right at the bottom underneath my Swiss army knife and the wooden pear I'd bought in yon new shop on Simpson Road. You know the one next to Ann Summers. That's the place with all the pants in the window. Senga had a look in there last week. She said I should take a peek inside and I might find something useful. She winked and tapped the side of her nose. I'll give it a try but their pants only seem to come in small sizes. Anyway I found my notebook. I turned to the right page and stood up.

"The bird is on the wing they say
But I think that's absurd
For surely anyone can see
The wing is on the bird"

They all just sat there when I'd finished. Amyamy had her mouth open and was staring at me.

Eventually she said, "This is a joke, right?" She sounded a bit nervous and sort of half smiled.

"It is a bit funny, I suppose," I said.

She burst out laughing and everyone joined in. I didn't think it was *that* funny but at least they had enjoyed it. It's nice to see people enjoying themselves.

"I can read you another one," I said.

"I'm sure we'd love to hear that, Seline, but..."

"The hens were outside clucking
While the farmer's wife was..."

"I think Seline that we should leave it there and give someone else a chance, don't you?"

"Of course," I said, although I thought it was a little rude of her to interrupt. It's not a long poem and the punch line is good.

The man with grey hair beside me stood up and said he had a poem to read out. He called it a high cow. I didn't understand what he meant. The poem was very short and had no rhyme at all. I don't think he'd put much effort into it and it had nothing to do with farming but Amyamy liked it. It's a good thing we're all different and like different things. 'Just as well we're not all like you, Seline,' Mam used to say.

"Can you tell me where the toilets are?" I whispered to him when he sat down. "I need to go."

"Just down stairs and on the left," he whispered.

I stood up and said, "I've got to go."

"Please, Seline, you must take your turn and not interrupt." She was going quite red in the face.

"No, I need to go to the toilet. It's my bladder, see. Doctor Campbell says..."

"Yes, yes." She waved her hand in the air. "Please go."

I stopped at the door. I didn't want her to get the wrong idea. "It's the excess pressure see and they had to twist the..."

"Seline, please. Please go."

She was an awful one for interrupting. I opened the door.

"Can I read another poem when..."

"Yes, yes. Well...yes. Just go."

The rest of the group had started muttering among themselves.

"I'll be back in five minutes."

She had started another coughing fit so I left. I found the loos easy. I'd been in there for a couple of minutes, it takes me a while see due to the twisting, when there was a noise outside. There were people clattering down the stairs and talking. Someone said "Ssssh". Quite right too. People are so inconsiderate.

When I finished I headed upstairs again but the man at the desk shouted after me.

"Oi, you're wastin' your time, doll."

"I am not," I said. "Writing's creative and other things."

"Well they've gone."

"Gone?"

"Gone home, finished early. Prior commitments the dragon said."

I looked at my watch. It was only 8.30. They'd finished an hour early.

"She never told me."

"Well I told yer, didn't I? Shower of loonies they are. Pure dead barking."

Oh well, perhaps I will try tapestry next week. I'm a dab hand with buttons. It's amazing what you can do with a needle and thread.

A Call for Paul

Life was good. "And it's getting better," I shouted to Susie in her cubby-hole. She appeared at the door, nail file in hand.

"What's that, Paul?"

"I said you get sexier every day, babe."

"Sod off. That's harassment," she pouted.

"Any time you like Susie, just say the word."

She raised one finger and wriggled back to her desk but came right back. "Anyway, there's a call for you. I put them on hold."

"What, when?"

"A... telephone... call... now," she said very slowly.

I picked up the phone. "Yes, but how long have they been..." I heard a click followed by what sounded like the heavy breathing of a hippo on heat at the other end.

"Good afternoon, Paul Plimsol here. How may I help you?"

The breathing stopped and there was complete silence for several seconds. I was just about to repeat myself when an odd voice rasped down the line.

"I've been waiting for ages you know. It's ridiculous."

"Yes, I'm sorry but..."

"And there was no music, nothing . The least you could do is give me a decent tune while my life seeps away never to be recovered in this life."

I forced myself to smile. "I am really sorry about the delay, we've got a new system in, it's causing us problems."

"It'll be a computer, they never work."

I felt like saying it was called Susie, and no, it didn't. "Anyway, sir, how may I assist you? Are you buying or selling?"

"What did you call me?"

What had I called him I tried desperately to think. Nothing. I didn't know his name. "I'm sorry, sir, I didn't catch your name. Mister...?"

"Mister nobody."

A joker - right. "Well, Mister Nobody, what can I do for you?"

"You're an impertinent young man, that's what you are. My uncle fought in the war for the likes of you. Well he would have if it hadn't been for his little habit. It's Seline Allbright."

Christ it was a woman. How could a woman have a voice like that? "I'm sorry Mrs Allbright..."

"It's Miss and don't you forget it. You youngsters are all the same, up all Saturday night with your loose moralities spewing all over the pavement. I've seen you."

"Look Miss Allbright, I can assure you..." Then I wondered if perhaps she had seen me. Best just carry on. "OK, can I help you? Can you at least tell me whether you are buying or selling?"

"Oh, I'm buying, dear. I'm looking for something a little bigger, well a lot bigger actually."

"Excellent, I'm sure we can help you. Spottiswoode and Dick are well known in..."

"Wooden what, dear?"

"Wooden... look why don't you make an appointment to come round and we can discuss your requirements?"

"I haven't any time for that. Have you got something big?"

"We have several five bedroom properties."

"Five bedrooms. What would I do with five bedrooms? Are you trying to insulate something? I'm a respectabled woman I don't go in for these orgy-borgies that everyone's at these days. It's disgusting. I read about it in the paper. They all need neutralising that's what."

I was beginning to feel quite weak. I would have sat down if I hadn't already been sitting down.

"I'm sorry, Miss Allbright it was just that you said you were looking for a large property."

"A large garage, I'm looking for, just like I told you. Bedrooms don't matter; I must have a big garage, with a flat roof."

"That's not what you..."

"What? What was that?"

"Nothing, nothing. I think I understand your requirements. It's still best if you come round..."

"Look, have you got something or not? There's plenty more fish in the pan."

I thought desperately. "There's a property in Albany Street. I could meet you there."

"Fine, two o'clock." The phone went dead. My watch said one pm.

She was waiting for me at the front door. A small middle-aged woman in a yellow cardigan.

I took a deep breath, pulled my shoulders back and marched up to the door.

"Hello, Miss Allbright?" I held out my hand.

"I'm Miss Allbright," she said.

"That's what I..."

"You're just being silly again. But that's all right, I like a good laugh." She poked me hard in the stomach with an index finger.

I closed my eyes and counted to one and a half.

"My name is Paul Plimsol," I said through clenched teeth and a granite smile. "Shall we begin the viewing now?"

"Yes, and I wish you'd hurry up. I haven't got all day you know."

"Right... right," I lowered my voice and fumbled in my pocket for the keys. "This is one of the larger properties on our books with four bedrooms, a spacious lounge..."

"Oh don't bother with that, where's the garage?"

"The garage is at the back, you really want to see that first?" But I was wasting my breath as she was already scuttling round to the back of the house, swaying from side to side with a peculiar rolling motion. I followed her, slowly.

She was standing by the garage, arms folded with her cardigan pulled tightly round her. "It's perfect," she said.

"It can take three cars," I said.

"Ideal, just perfect."

"You have three cars?" I just couldn't stop myself. I knew it sounded cheeky but I was convinced that I was being strung along in some elaborate hoax.

"Cars, oh I don't have a car." She turned the handle and opened the up and over door.

I stared at her. "You don't have any cars?"

She blinked at me and for the first time I noticed that she had a squint in her left eye so that only one eye could focus on me at a time. "You're being silly again aren't you. What's the point in me having a car when I can't drive."

I rubbed my forehead with a sweaty hand. "You don't drive?"

"No dear... well not cars anyway." She had lowered her voice and glanced round furtively as if she wished she hadn't spoken.

I could hear the strident ringing of alarm bells somewhere at the back of my brain but even so I couldn't stop the words coming out. "You drive something else then, do you?"

She stared at me with her right eye then changed to her left while her right examined her nose. "You'll have to promise not to say."

"No, no it doesn't really matter. I think I'll have to get back to the office," I looked at my watch.

"It started with Mam you see. They took her like. One minute she was sitting in her chair puffing on her pipe, next thing she's gone."

"She died?"

"No, no they took her, the aliens."

"Aliens," I squeaked. I glanced round but there was no-one at the garage door. I took a tiny step backwards.

"Yes, she left a note, Dear Seline gone with the aliens. They say it's nicer on their planet. Dinners in the oven, ships in the box on the table. Remember to feed Fergie. See you around. Fergie was her venus flytrap."

I moved back again but she stepped towards me. Christ, she might have a knife under that cardigan.

"So..." My mind seemed to have frozen. "So you want a garage?"

"Yes, see this ship in the box on the table was like a little model but it kept getting bigger. Growing like a plant it was. In six months I had to take it outside. Covered it with some old sheets. I've been inside it now. I reckon I can fly it. But the neighbours are getting a bit funny so I need a garage for it and a flat roof to land and take off."

I was out of this. "Well there it is, perfect for you. I've got to go. It's Tuesday and things happen."

"It's Thursday."

"Yes, oh dear, there's even more on Thursday."

"I'll take the house," she shouted after me.

"Call the office," I yelled as I sprinted for my car.

"You're a rude man. I might just take my business elsewhere," was the last thing I heard her say.

Back at the office I collapsed at my desk.

"Susie doll, I need a cuddle."

She sniffed. "You need a bath, you stink."

I couldn't think of a reply. I put my hand out in front of me. It was trembling. That woman was mad. She might have done anything. I was lucky to get out of it. I was sure I would never hear from her again. I didn't. Not directly.

Evening Echo

18th July 2007

An explosion in a residential garage badly damaged two adjacent properties in Farewell Drive, Johnston last night. A police spokeswoman would not rule out terrorism as a possible cause. Local resident Enid Bradshaw (51) reported seeing a column of smoke disappearing into the sky, 'like one of them space rockets'.

In a separate incident in the neighbourhood police have arrested local estate agent Paul Plimsol (28) for breach of the peace. Residents had complained about him staggering around in an apparently drunken state, knocking on doors and repeatedly shouting 'she told me.'

Seline Saves the World

Seline Allbright's the name and it's quite a story.

One day the black Bedford pulled into Mr. McMaster's drive just where I couldn't see what was going on. By the time I rushed round the corner a guy in dark glasses was driving the van away. Next day the aerial went up. A huge thing it was. Like an umbrella on the end of a pole thirty feet tall. Evil Aliens, I thought. It seemed the logical conclusion. I knew I was going to bump into them sometime. I've studied them for long enough, read all the books Nancy in the library can get for me, and lots of people have seen them, so I wasn't surprised that they'd moved next door.

It was quite exciting really to know that Evil Aliens were living so close by. Mind you I've always been suspicious of Mrs. Simpson at Number eleven. Curtains tight shut at one o'clock in the afternoon. Really. Couldn't prove it though. If only I could speak to her - but she never answers the door. This was different.

Mr. McMaster had only moved in a month ago. He was a bit rude I thought when I called to say hello as the removal men started to unload the furniture. Tried to stop me getting into the van. But I made allowances. Now I could see why. There was probably lots he didn't want me to see.

What should I do? Call the police? They probably knew all about the alien and had been mind wiped or wouldn't believe me. Last time I phoned they didn't even bother to come round. I had to walk all the way to the station in the rain. The sergeant was a nasty piece of work. Just a bully, talking to me like that, a law abiding citizen, just because I dripped on his notepad and made the ink run. Anyway since he told me that he had my number I've been waiting for him to call.

OK, Seline you're on your own I said. I would go and speak to the Alien. Funny how aliens are always male. I guess they must leave their wives at home while they terrorise the universe and wipe out civilisation. I suppose terrorising and wiping out is just one of those male things. I wasn't scared. I've seen him in Safeway buying washing powder and I was sure he wouldn't kill me in the middle of the day. I'd have to make sure my door was locked tonight of course. I put on my blue cardie.

I marched round the corner into Rodney Drive instead of taking the quickest way over the fence. I knew from experience that people preferred to have a knock at their front door. I knocked at the front door.

Mr. McMaster opened the door. He stood staring at me, his mouth hanging open, a strange expression on his face. I'm sure he didn't expect me. He was wearing pink piggy slippers. I'll bet he felt guilty. He looked upwards at something above the door frame that I couldn't see. A trap? I stepped inside and looked up too but I could only see the blank wall. He developed a coughing fit. Just a pretext to cover his confusion I think.

"Can I help you?" he finally managed to say, standing right in front of me so that I couldn't see past him.

Now I must admit that I wasn't quite sure what I was gong to do. Play it by ear is always my motto. It's never worth planning much ahead, I find, things change so quickly. I was going to have to rely on my wits. I remember Mam used to say, "Seline, with your wits and my muscles we make a good team." She wasn't that strong so I had to think doubly hard.

"No, not really," I said. "I'm your neighbour from across the fence, you know, I just wondered..." What had I wondered? This was tricky.

"I know," he said. His voice sounded very flat. He was examining the ceiling in close detail again. His cheeks flushed. Definitely guilty about something I thought.

Inspiration struck. "I wondered if you'd noticed that big aerial thing in your garden?"

"Noticed it." He paused to cough again. "Of course I noticed it. It's mine. I put it up myself."

No pretence. At least he was honest. "That's good." I said.

He stared at me. His eyes were all sort of bulgy and watery. There was silence for a few moments. I could hear a clock striking in a room somewhere behind him. It had a very pleasant ding.

"Is that it," he blustered.

"Yes, ten o'clock. I suppose it's an antique." I said.

His hand was on his forehead, rubbing hard. Perhaps a subcutaneous communication implant. I had no doubt that our conversation was now being recorded for training purposes. Perhaps even transmitted live.

"It's not an antique. How could it be an antique? I've only just bought it."

I knew right away he was talking about the aerial again. Just couldn't keep away from the subject.

"Please go," he said.

Now that was tricky. What exactly did he mean? I was sure there was something significant behind those words. Play for time Seline, I told myself.

"I like aerials," I lied. "There's something about them. A certain je ne sais what."

"What?"

"It's French." I almost felt sorry for him. It must be difficult with all the worlds' languages to learn. "Can you speak Chinese?"

He was shaking his head. "I don't understand you. Why don't you leave me alone? What do you want?"

"Well I just wanted to see your aerial and all the other stuff. I bet there's lots of other stuff." I darted my head to the side to try and see round him.

"Don't tell me you're interested in radio?"

"Yes, that's it. Radio's my thing I'm always listening. There's always something on."

He gave a huge sigh. "I suppose you'd better come and look if it will keep you happy."

I felt that I'd carried that off really well. This was dangerous. Into the lion's den and all that. I'm sure he wasn't as stupid as he looked.

He slammed the front door shut and led me to a door at the back of the hall and threw it open. "There you are."

I gasped. The room was crammed from top to bottom with stuff. Computers and things with dials and switches. Things with winking red and green lights. Humming things, flashing things. The nerve centre obviously. Why was he showing me this? Be subtle, Seline, I told myself.

"Why are you showing me this?" I said.

"You wanted to see it, dear. It's what I do. It's my hobby."

His hobby indeed! Destroying planets and subjugating the human race a hobby. I ask you. No point in pleading with him then. Pitiless he was. No feelings. I felt calm though. Direct action was called for..

"Got any tea?" I asked.

He looked at me funny like.

"Tea. You've got a cheek."

"Yes," I said. What did he mean by that?

"Look if I give you a cup of tea, will you go away?"

"Yes, of course," I said. I smiled at him as nicely as I could.

He made a funny noise and marched to the door. "Come on then. I'm not leaving you in here on your own." Damn! How had he seen through my plan?

I only took a sip of the tea. I knew it was drugged.

"Thank you," I said. "I'll see you later."

"In your dreams," he said.

More like my nightmares.

And then I was outside. I'd escaped. I looked at the blue sky and the lovely trees and the little birds and all the beautiful things on this beautiful planet that's home to me now and I knew what I had to do.

Preparations first. I made the emergency call to Alpha Centauri. The one I hoped I would never have to make. It's easy, you just press the buttons on the radio in the right order. Two, one, five, six. Just like my telephone number. It's not really a radio of course, it's a sub ethereal communication device but nobody knows that but me. My pals on AC will help me if the Evil Alien overpowers me.

So that's it. I've written it all down in case I don't come back. I'm going there tonight when it's dark and this time I'll make sure. I'll take all the gear, knives, hammers, disrupter beams. I think that he knows that I know about him, but does he know about me? You know what they say. It takes one to know one. I've been waiting a long time to fulfil my destiny. They put me here you see to deliver the human race from the Evil Alien Hordes. I remember what Mam said.

"You must be meant for something in life, Seline. Christ knows what."

All these years I've been waiting for him to let me know the moment and now he has.

****

The Daily Record 16th Sep 2009
Gas Explosion Rocks Rodney Drive

An explosion last night completely demolished a house in Rodney Drive, West London. All that remains of the £90000 house is a smoking hole in the ground. Police are unsure if the house was occupied. Miraculously the houses on each side were completely unscathed although several people are being treated for shock. Police have ruled out terrorist activity and the most likely cause is a gas explosion. Reporter Andy Coltstooth interviewed a resident, Miss. Allbright(58) who claimed to have witnessed the explosion.

"I seen it all. A white light from the sky it was. And a noise like to blow your socks off. I didn't get there in time you see. Too slow, so they done it for me." Miss Allbright was off the opinion that the explosion was the work of little green men from Mars. Your reporter thinks the local gas company should continue its investigation!!

****

Report to comsec &&aleph-cent.&&

Sig received red-red deep agent 2NZ repeat red-red.

All traffic on hold. Plan terraxtrem in operation. All agent alert. Report soonest.

****